Roman Empire Power and People

Dirk Booms,
Belinda Crerar
and Susan Raikes

The British
Museum

This book is published to accompany the touring exhibition
Roman Empire: Power and People at Bristol Museum and Art
Gallery from 21 September to 5 January 2013; Norwich Castle
Museum and Art Gallery from 25 January 2013 to 27 April 2014;
Herbert Art Gallery & Museum from 17 May to 31 August 2014;
and Tyne & Wear Archives & Museums from 30 May to
13 September 2015.

Dirk Booms, Belinda Crerar and Susan Raikes have asserted the
right to be identified as the authors of this work.

First published in 2013 by The British Museum Press
A division of The British Museum Company Ltd
38 Russell Square, London WC1B 3QQ
britishmuseum.org/publishing

A catalogue record for this book is available
from the British Library
ISBN: 978-0-7141-2285-4

Designed by Bobby Birchall, Bobby and Co.
Printed in China by 1010 Printing International Ltd

The papers used by the British Museum Press are recyclable
products and the manufacturing processes are expected to
conform to the environmental regulations of the country of origin.

The majority of objects illustrated in this book are from the
collection of the British Museum. Registration numbers are listed
in the image credits on page 155. You can find out more about
objects in all areas of the British Museum's collection on the
Museum's website at:
britishmuseum.org/research/search_the_collection_database.aspx

Frontispiece: Panel decorated with Roman and Dacian armour,
probably based on the sculptured decoration of the base of
Trajan's Column, erected in Rome to commemorate Trajan's
victorious campaigns against the Dacians. Rome, 2nd century AD.
Marble, H. 81.3 cm, W. 83.8 cm.

CONTENTS

INTRODUCTION

'LOOK CLOSELY AT THE PAST AND ITS CHANGING
EMPIRES, AND IT IS POSSIBLE TO FORESEE
THE THINGS TO COME.'

MARCUS AURELIUS, *MEDITATIONS* 7.27

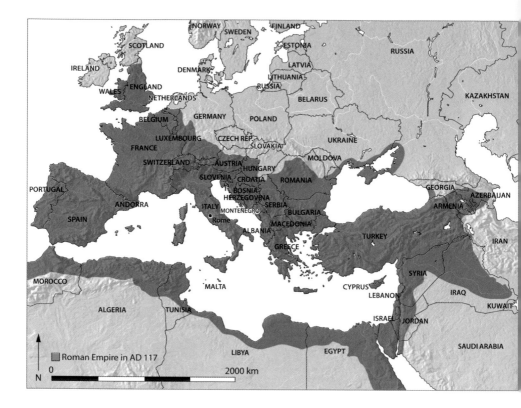

AT THE HEIGHT of its power, the Roman Empire stretched from Spain to Iraq and from the North Sea to the southern border of Egypt, encompassing all the territory in between. By AD 117, it had engulfed the area of around fifty modern-day countries. The history of the world has been dominated by such empires, from the dynasties of China to the Maya of Central America and, more recently, the British Empire. But none has left a more lasting impact on the culture of Europe than that of the Romans. From the languages spoken, the legal systems in place and the development of towns, to the taste for wine and use of dinner plates, the enduring legacy of the Romans continues to reverberate in the day-to-day life of Europeans. Following in Alexander's footsteps, Rome introduced temperate Europe, North Africa and parts of the Near East to its way of life – and the rest, as they say, is history.

Above: The modern countries that now cover the area of the Roman Empire during the reign of Trajan (AD 98–117). A map showing specific cities mentioned can be found on page 152.

Opposite: This flask in the form of the Egyptian goddess Isis was made in Knidos, modern Turkey, but was found in Hama, Syria, symbolizing the multi-cultural aspects of the Roman Empire. AD 60–100. Terracotta, L. 35.7 cm.

In this book, we explore how being part of the Roman Empire changed people's lives. Already by the end of the first century AD the term 'Roman' had taken on a completely different meaning from denoting a place of birth or residence, and included myriads of people with very different origins and cultural backgrounds. We will look at how particular people identified themselves in their part of the empire, but also how they were seen and identified by others. Certain unifying changes, such as the formal organization of cities and the use of the Latin language, would have made all corners of the empire feel familiar to any traveller, but local traditions proved tenacious and were even encouraged by Rome itself. This brought variety and vibrancy to the provinces, but with it, ethnic tensions and cultural arrogance. Appreciating how people reacted to the confrontation with Rome through their art, religion, fashion and burial customs allows us to see the Roman Empire not just as a monolithic top-down vehicle of oppression and exploitation, but as a diverse array of cultural interactions, adoptions and exchanges. Equally, cultural influence was not a one-way affair – Rome itself embraced gods, food and even emperors sent back from its new territories. 'Being Roman' was thus not simply a matter of provincial peoples adopting fashions and attitudes from the conquerors. Traditions persisted and local heritage was valued in the face of overwhelming change.

Our knowledge of the Roman Empire comes through a combination of texts and material remains, lost, buried, discarded or even handed down for almost two thousand years. Roman historians and bureaucrats tell us about encounters with new peoples and their dealings with alien cultures, of which they did not always approve. Obviously, such texts only tell us one side of the story. What of the ordinary people? Sometimes we hear their voices too, through the letters of soldiers written on papyrus from Egypt, thanking native gods but signing off with their newly adopted Roman name, or complaining about the miserable British weather at Hadrian's Wall and asking for more beer. Yet more often, it is the objects which they made and left behind that can tell us about their beliefs, their concerns, their values and their ambitions. Figures of Egyptian gods dressed in Roman military armour and the widespread trade in Roman tableware, which was used alongside local pottery both within the empire and beyond its frontiers, impress upon us the vast influence of Rome on the lives of its subjects and the persistence of inherent traditions within its territories.

Above: A striped, woollen child's sock. Preserved by the arid conditions of the desert, this everyday item from Roman Egypt offers a rare insight into daily life. El-Sheikh Ibada, AD 200–400. Wool, L. 12.3 cm, W. 6.4 cm.

Opposite: Figure of the Egyptian falcon god Horus wearing Roman military dress. Egypt, Roman period. Painted limestone, H. 54.5 cm, W. 31.8 cm.

The wide-ranging collection of the British Museum includes objects from every outpost of the Roman Empire. They offer a remarkable opportunity to highlight how cultural influences moved between provinces, both in cases where local traditions and customs continued alongside those imported from Rome, and where the distinctions between the two became blurred. Two thousand years later, we will never be able to answer perfectly the questions these objects raise about how far non-Roman cultures were integrated, altered or swept away, and even less understand indigenous concerns about all the changes. Nevertheless, history and archaeology have provided countless tantalizing clues.

PART I:
POWER

CHAPTER 1

POWER AND GLORY

ROME GREW from a collection of hilltop hamlets by a strategic point on the river Tiber in the tenth century BC, and the Romans shared the Italian peninsula with numerous other peoples including the Etruscans, Sabines and Samnites in central Italy, and the Greeks in the south and in Sicily. However, from the fourth century BC onwards, the city sought to expand its territories and, with it, to take control over these other peoples, either by treaties or by direct war. One by one during the second half of the third century BC, the non-Roman cities in Italy fell to Roman conquest and their peoples were assimilated into Roman culture, either as citizens, allies or slaves. Sicily was to become the first Roman province, as early as 241 BC, and from that very first moment was seen as a possession rather than an ally. Cicero tells us that centuries later this same sentiment was still felt – that Sicily was 'the first to teach our ancestors how wonderful it is to rule foreign peoples' (Cicero, *Against Verres* 2.2).

The conquest of Sicily was also, according to the historian Livy (*History of Rome* 25.40.2), the very first moment that Romans encountered Greek works of art, and it marked the beginning of their sometimes difficult love affair with Greek culture. Subsequent conquests only strengthened their interest in Hellenic art and culture: the Greek peninsula was conquered in 146 BC and the Hellenistic Attalid kingdom of Pergamon in the western part of Asia Minor (modern-day Turkey) was bequeathed to them in 133 BC by its last king Attalus III, to avoid both a succession crisis and major bloodshed. From then onwards, the luxuries encountered in these and other Hellenistic kingdoms started to permeate into every aspect of Roman daily life. Obviously, such extravagances were not for everyone, and it was the elite who enjoyed them in the first place. During the Republic, these were the richest members of society who often also held the most important political positions. However, with the accession of the first emperor Augustus in 27 BC, the newest luxuries were introduced first at the court, amongst the imperial family and the closest of the emperor's friends, and only then moved through the lower levels of the elite. Among all those desirable items, the Romans took a specific liking to two types of material, marble and glass. They not only adopted these from the east, but they also perfected their uses and trade, and as such, marble and glass became symbols of Roman life, both in Rome itself and in its provinces.

Glass in particular flowed down the lines of hierarchy in Roman society, with the newest, most beautiful and technologically most advanced products first reaching the emperor and the highest elite. These would be objects like the beautiful Portland Vase, now in the British Museum, blown in layers of differently coloured glass at a workshop in Rome from which only a handful of almost complete vessels have survived. But when glass predictably became more common, the upper echelons of society had to search repeatedly for new products to maintain their exclusive reputation. Two such objects in the Museum's collection, the Barber and Crawford cups, are the only known vessels of their kind from antiquity. These were carved from the mineral fluorite (or fluorspar) and were so rare

Below: The Crawford Cup, carved from fluorite and similar to one for which the emperor Nero paid 1 million sesterces. Turkey, AD 50–100. Fluorite, H. 9.7 cm, W. 14.9 cm, Diam. 10.7 cm.

and popular that the emperor Nero is said to have paid 1 million *sesterces* for just one of them, the equivalent of more than a thousand times the yearly salary of the average soldier (Pliny, *Natural History* 37.18–22).

White marble, on the other hand, had been used in Greece and Asia Minor for centuries, both for statues and for architecture, especially temples. The Romans were greatly impressed by its characteristics and started employing the material for their own uses. However, encountering several quarries of other stones in the conquered areas, they specifically took a liking to coloured marbles, and these are perhaps the most eye-catching among the remains of many ruins or standing buildings today: yellow marble from Tunisia, green and red marble from Greece, pink granite and purple porphyry from Egypt and so on. The demand for these coloured stones reached

*Opposite top:
Dedicatory altar
of Primigenius
Iuvencianus. He was
a scribe in the marble
trade in Rome under
and for Vespasian, and
is thus likely to have
overseen the import
of columns and other
marble fragments for
the construction of the
Colosseum. Rome,
AD 69–79. Marble,
H. 72 cm, W. 46 cm,
D. 30 cm.*

*Opposite bottom:
Reconstruction of
Nero's Domus Aurea
by Jean-Claude
Golvin. Built after the
fire of AD 64, which
destroyed large parts
of Rome, it dominated
the centre of the city.*

*Right: Fragment of
a wall painting from
Nero's Domus Aurea,
showing a Greek-style
caryatid with long
ringlets of dark hair.
Rome, AD 54–68.
Painted plaster,
H. 32 cm, W 25.5 cm.*

such heights that they not only became one of the most organized trades in the empire but also one of the most profitable, and in time all the quarries became private possessions of the emperor himself.

The story of Nero's fluorite cup is typical in that it tells us that the grandest examples of the opulence and architecture from the Roman Empire can be found at the houses and villas of the emperors themselves. Two such complexes dwarfed all others: Nero's palace in Rome, already known then as the Domus Aurea ('Golden House'), and Hadrian's villa in Tivoli (p. 21), about 30 kilometres from Rome, which was the same size (and had the same number of buildings) as a small city. The Domus

Aurea occupied a large part of the centre of Rome, and the emperor spared no expense in embellishing it with every type of luxury possible. Tellingly, it is one of the few building complexes of that time for which we know both the architects, Severus and Celer, and the painter of its elaborate gilded wall paintings, Fabullus. Never before had an emperor so blatantly indulged himself, and for some of his contemporaries this was a step too far. Popular feelings ranged from awe to disgust:

> Nero took advantage of the country's desolation and built a palace in which the jewels and the gold, already rendered ordinary by our extravagance, were even less marvellous than the fields and the lakes, with forests on one side to resemble inaccessible wilderness, and open spaces and wide views on the other.
> (Tacitus, *Annals* 15.42.1)

> All parts were overlaid with gold, gemstones and mother-of-pearl. The dining rooms had ivory-panelled ceilings: they could rotate to shower the guests with flowers, and they contained tubes to sprinkle perfume. The main, circular dining hall revolved day and night,

Above: Fragment of a gilded wall painting from Nero's Domus Aurea, showing a frieze with a pair of sphinxes amongst acanthus plants, and the myth of Leda and the swan in the roundels. Rome, AD 54–68. Painted plaster, gilding, L. 39 cm, W. 16.5 cm.

Opposite top: Reconstruction of Hadrian's villa in Tivoli by Jean-Claude Golvin.

Opposite below: The so-called 'Capri Altar' is an 18th-century composition using fragments of an original Roman majestic candle holder. The scenes evoke pastoral landscapes. It probably comes from Tiberius' sumptuous villa on the island of Capri. Naples, 1st century AD. Marble, H. 69.8 cm.

imitating the skies ... When the palace was finished and Nero dedicated it, the only approval he gave was by saying that at last he was housed like a human being.
(Suetonius, *Nero* 31.2)

Although Hadrian's villa in Tivoli surpassed the Domus Aurea both in size and in luxury, the emperor was more widely respected than Nero and criticism was relatively low (and of course, his villa wasn't right in the middle of Rome). It is thought that different parts of the villa represented places and provinces that the emperor visited on his extensive travels through 'his' empire, and we especially find references to Greek and Egyptian buildings and landscapes. Accordingly, the grounds were littered with Greek statues brought over to Rome, Roman versions of Greek originals, as well as new Roman ones. To decorate the floors and walls in elaborate, geometrical patterns, dozens of differently coloured marbles were used, thought also to represent the different provinces that they came from. Sometimes the already costly marble in these panels was replaced by even more expensive

Opposite: The Pantheon: probably the best preserved Roman building today, the dome being one of the empire's masterpieces of engineering.

Above: This glass-inlaid tile is one of the most luxurious found in the Roman Empire. They were discovered in the imperial villa at Acquatraversa near Rome, which belonged to the emperor Lucius Verus. Mid-2nd century AD. Glass, L. 11.1 cm.

glass imitations, perhaps in an ultimate attempt to impress visitors and outdo peers when marble decoration became too common. Combined with the Roman drive for architectural experimentation, the resulting buildings often include different varieties of dome, thought to have been designed by the emperor himself and very similar to the great dome of the best preserved Roman building today, the Pantheon in Rome, also largely constructed under Hadrian.

This impressive architecture and accompanying luxury visible everywhere in the capital of such a vast empire must surely have impressed any visitor from the provinces, and must have formed the core of any memories that they had of the capital. It is therefore no surprise that we find imitations of some of Rome's most evocative buildings in the richer and technologically more advanced regions of the empire. Augustus' temple of Mars Ultor became a standard model for temples, with copies in the south of France, Spain and Asia Minor, and a miniature Pantheon was built in Pergamon. Palaces in Roman Britain (Fishbourne) and Spain (Tarragona), as well as a handful of villas of the wealthy in France, Germany and Spain show the remains of imported marbles used to imitate the marble wall and floor decorations of Italy. However, in most regions of the empire, sculpture and architecture from Rome was impossible to import, for both financial and logistical reasons. Every other type of luxury product, however, be it glass, ceramics, textiles, exotic foodstuffs or even the techniques for executing wall paintings, was disseminated to the remotest areas in the empire, and these will be explored further throughout this book.

To conquer an empire as vast as this and, more crucially, maintain power over it, the Romans depended heavily on a large professional army. In the early days, Rome only recruited soldiers for specific campaigns, and only from those citizens who were able to afford their own armour (meaning that they were not highly trained), and then disbanded the armies when the campaign finished. However, important reforms in the last century of the Republic, and further ones by Augustus, resulted in the creation of a permanent professional army that would continue to exist, albeit in a variety of forms and sizes, for many centuries.

Left: Bust of a woman, possibly Artemis, from Hadrian's villa in Tivoli. 2nd century AD. Marble, H. (original) 33 cm, (with modern bust) 65 cm.

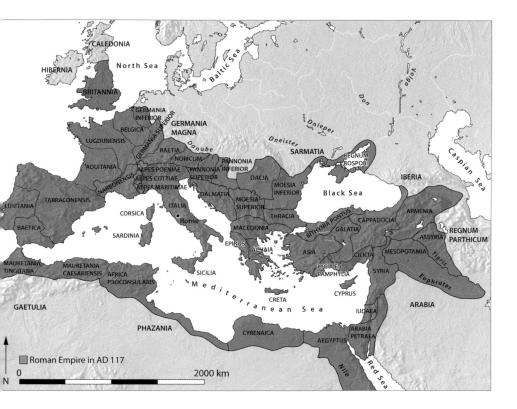

Above: At its maximum expansion in AD 117, the Roman Empire contained forty-five provinces of various sizes, as well as Italy itself.

The Roman army at its largest, around AD 200, consisted of thirty-three legions of highly trained infantry, each of some 5,500 soldiers (all Roman citizens), plus 400 auxiliary regiments (of non-Romans, mostly from the provinces of the empire), representing about 225,000 troops, which included the cavalry, archers, slingers, camel riders, scouts and numerous other specially trained fighters: a total of more than 400,000 soldiers. Rome's great achievement was to recognize the fighting prowess of the cultures it overthrew and rather than disbanding these forces, to harness their specialist skills and use them to its own advantage. The cosmopolitan composition of this vast army is discussed further later in this book.

An ordinary legionary soldier carried a javelin and a shield and wore a distinctive helmet, examples of which have been found all over the empire, often only with minor variations. One particularly successful military technique was the so-called *testudo* or tortoise formation, though it was slow, clumsy and difficult to maintain for long periods of time. A band of soldiers interlocked their large, rectangular shields to form a complete barricade around themselves and hidden under this 'shell' they could advance forward impervious to most missiles. An unknown author tells us that Caesar used it against Pompey's army at Ruspina, now in Tunisia, in 46 BC, and it is also mentioned by Plutarch as having been used by Marc Antony in the wars against Parthia. It was depicted on Trajan's famous victory column, which stands 30 metres high in the centre of Rome and is adorned with a tour-de-force of carved scenes telling the story of the Dacian wars, implying that the *testudo* was a signature manoeuvre and a familiar sight within the Roman army.

With such numbers, weaponry and tactics, it is no surprise that the empire continued to expand. Julius Caesar brought about the conquests of most of Gaul (modern France and Belgium) and parts of Germany, but the most vigorous expansion occurred under Augustus with the conquests of Egypt, southern and central Turkey, and parts of Spain and eastern Europe. Claudius famously invaded Britain, while Trajan added further provinces in the east.

Above: A standard type of shield of the Roman Empire, found as far away from the capital as possible, at its furthest boundary in Dura Europos (modern Syria). Mid-3rd century AD. Painted wood and rawhide, H. 105.5 cm, W. 41 cm.

Left: Gilded bronze helmet made in the Danube Valley in the 3rd century AD. It was purely ceremonial and far too delicate to have ever been used in battle. Austria, c. AD 200–250. Gold and copper alloy, H. 25 cm, W. 20.2 cm, D. 22.5 cm.

Above: This scene from Trajan's Column in Rome shows Roman legionaries using the tortoise formation. Plaster cast of a marble original from Rome, c. AD 113.

During Trajan's reign, the Roman Empire was at its largest, encompassing forty-five provinces, the equivalent of around fifty modern countries. These annexed provinces varied wildly in size and population, and were roughly distinguished along tribal or cultural lines as they had been

before the Roman conquest. For example, the province of Gallia Belgica included all the peoples who were identified as Belgae, and Raetia (northern Italy, southern Germany and Switzerland) included all the different Raetian tribes. However, sometimes related peoples ended up in different provinces, either when a province was just too big or was awkwardly positioned, as in the case of Germania which was split in two and named Upper and Lower Germania (Germania Superior and Inferior), or when different parts of one homogenous area joined the empire at different times, as happened in Asia Minor (modern Turkey), which was divided into six different provinces.

The consolidation and defence of such a vast empire was a constant worry, and therefore armies were not only employed to fight, but were also stationed, sometimes permanently, throughout the empire for defence and as a deterrent against hostile forces. Upon arrival at a frontier zone, soldiers would immediately start building a temporary wooden fort, which, if it continued to be used, was upgraded to a permanent stone construction.

Above: During expeditions, the legionaries could erect a temporary fort in just a few hours. This scene from Trajan's Column in Rome depicts such construction during the wars in Dacia. Rome, c. AD 113, marble.

Right: A reconstruction of Hadrian's Wall.

Below: Hadrian's Wall today: one of the most impressive surviving remains of the Roman Empire in Britain.

Again on Trajan's Column, the scene of building temporary fortresses or fortifications is repeated no less than six times, clearly indicating its standardization when going on campaign. These forts largely took the same iconic form in whichever province they were created, adapted slightly to the lie of the land. Their plan resembled that of the early cities that Rome founded as colonies in Italy: rectangular, with a perpendicular street grid and with the forum and

most important administrative buildings at the junction of
the two main roads. The plans of these cities and of the
forts is thought to have been specifically designed by the
Roman Senate as the 'ideal Roman city', and the use of
this model in the provinces has been seen as a deliberate
dissemination of Roman 'fashions' and ideology. In fact,
many elements of these forts survive today, their stone
remains and streets incorporated in modern city plans or
buildings. For example, at Chester the four main roads
of the modern town, Bridge Street, Northgate Street,
Eastgate Street and Watergate Street, not only preserve
the trajectories of the main arteries of the fortress, but also
allude to the gates to which they led.

Furthermore, when new towns were built to reward the
large number of army veterans with land (a practice that
started in Italy during the Republic and continued in the

*Above: The
reconstructed
entrance gates to
the legionary fort
at Arbeia (South
Shields) on Hadrian's
Wall.*

provinces for centuries) the same plan was used, possibly because this is what the soldiers were accustomed to. It may also have reflected ideological concerns about rationality, symmetry and dominance over the landscape, and it could be adapted to the existing hierarchy among lower and higher ranking veterans, as the latter might have received a double plot of land. The best surviving example of such a town is Timgad, a Pompeii-like city in modern Algeria, because it was preserved by the Saharan sands after it was abandoned. Despite not being fortified, the town is strictly rectangular in shape and the internal area is divided into uniform blocks separated by entirely straight roads. Apart from the plan, several of the building types within forts (such as the forum or central square, temples and baths) were also standardized throughout the empire. Even a superficial comparison between the city gates of Arbeia on Hadrian's Wall and Xanten on the German frontier shows that they were practically identical. In the provinces that lacked a monumental architecture of their own (in western Europe, but also North Africa and some eastern provinces), the power

Below: The reconstructed entrance gates to the legionary fort at Colonia Ulpia Traiana (modern Xanten), Germany.

of Rome was made all the more apparent through this imposing and alien architecture.

Another building type was the amphitheatre, rarely built within the forts, but without a doubt linked to them and to the arrival of the military in a new province. While theatres were a Greek invention that was adopted by the Romans, the amphitheatre was a newly created building type for an early Etruscan and Roman practice, namely gladiatorial fights carried out as part of the funerary rites. It is easy to understand why gladiatorial games were popular among the soldiers and the army, and it is through the military stationing in Rome's provinces that the games and

Below: Oil lamp in the form of a gladiator's helmet. Oil lamps were found throughout Roman society and depict the most popular subjects of the day. London, mid-1st century AD. Pottery, H. 8.2 cm, W. 8.6 cm, D. 8.3 cm.

Above: Marble carving depicting fighting gladiators. This relief was found in Ephesus, one of the cities in Asia Minor that had a large immigrant population of Romans. Ephesus, 1st–2nd century AD. Marble, H. 75.9 cm, W. 41.9 cm.

the building of amphitheatres spread to the local populations. It is therefore no surprise to find depictions of gladiators all over the empire, on small objects such as lamps or statuettes, to large reliefs and mosaics that commemorated famous games or famous gladiators who, with enough successful fights under their belts, could become the celebrities of the ancient world. However, the degree to which gladiatorial games were popular varies from province to province: in Britain, North Africa and especially Gaul they were adopted with enthusiasm, while in Greece and Turkey scarcely any amphitheatres have been discovered. This is partly because gladiatorial games were put on in existing structures in those provinces, but it also betrays an underlying reluctance towards such games from these Hellenized populations, which we find in the writings of people such as Dio Chrysostom, Lucian, Philostratus or even the emperor Julian. Since gladiatorial games in these provinces were part of the Imperial cult, they were associated by the inhabitants and many others with a threat to Greek culture, a not-too-subtle way for the Romans to impose their own customs, as well as a gratuitous blood-shedding. It is no coincidence that most of the evidence for gladiatorial games in Greece and Turkey, be it architectural or literary, comes from places with either high levels of Roman immigrants or with a prominent Imperial cult, such as Athens, Corinth, Halicarnassus, Aphrodisias, Pergamon and especially Ephesus, where recently a large gladiator cemetery was discovered. In general, Greece and Asia Minor held on to their indigenous traditions more than most other provinces: they continued to speak Greek and kept their own customs and beliefs. From this vantage point the presence of amphitheatres and gladiatorial games could be seen as a measure of how much a city wanted to look or act Roman, or please the emperor.

Above: An antefix found at Holt, a Roman fort in Wales, with an inscription of the Legio XX Valeria Victrix, who made it for the building of its permanent fort. Wrexham, 2nd–3rd century AD. Terracotta, H. 21 cm.

Together with a typical Roman city plan and typical Roman building types, Roman construction techniques and sculptural tastes were also imported into the provinces when the army appeared. A good example of this is the introduction of fired brick as a building material into Britannia, where this type of construction was unknown previously: many tiles still bear the stamps of the legions that made them. Similarly, the appearance of Roman-style decorated architectural elements and sculpture is also often linked to the arrival of the army or, more likely, to the arrival of higher status Roman citizens who joined the military campaigns, either as commanders or as merchants. A military campaign was an excellent opportunity to explore new markets for the shrewd businessman. However, since such objects could only be imported from Italy with much difficulty, unlike glass or pottery, what we find in the provinces are local variants, made from local materials and perhaps, but not necessarily, by local craftsmen. The results, therefore, combine Roman models and local style, and whether this was because of an inability to fully imitate Roman originals or a desire to retain elements of native heritage remains a hotly debated issue in modern archaeological research.

Right: Sandstone head found in London. Traces of plaster on the surface indicate that the facial features were built up with plaster applied to the inner stone core. London, mid-1st–4th century AD. H. 33.5 cm, W. 15.3 cm.

Below: Marble head of a man. Colchester, probably dating to the 3rd century AD. H. 26 cm, W. 10.5 cm.

Such is the debate over a sandstone head that still shows traces of the plaster that was used for the finer facial features (right). While it is possible that this technique was used because it might have been difficult for either classically-trained Romans or local craftsmen to carve in limestone, it could equally be a remnant of an indigenous style of sculpture. Similarly, a sculpted head from Britain of a man (below), possibly dating to the third century AD, shows crude workmanship compared to marble examples in Rome. The same rudimentary workmanship is visible in the finishing of two new architectural motifs introduced to pre-Roman Britain, a decorated column and a decorative vase, both found in London (overleaf). These could equally well be the product of a local craftsman trying to imitate something that could only have been described to him verbally, or of a Roman sculptor, unfamiliar with the type of stone he had to work with.

As discussed earlier, permanent forts were built throughout the empire, but they were especially necessary at the borders, the so-called *limites* (singular: *limes*), where in some of the provinces it was even felt necessary to build a continuous wall. However, these physical boundaries should not be seen as evidence that the empire was under constant and large-scale attack. Instead, they both offered protection from smaller attacks and deterred potential threats, and acted as surveillance and signal posts. On the whole, borders were only partially manned.

In fact, the creation of a defensive infrastructure with small look-out teams at the borders made it possible for the rest of the army to move around the provinces or the interior of the empire more effectively, especially in times of low risk. But at the first indication that a large-scale attack was coming, troops could be deployed to the region under threat to strengthen the defence. It is estimated that only 3,000 troops were stationed on Hadrian's Wall, at fortlets 1.6 kilometres apart, but in times of threat they could be backed up by a force of another 25,000 men.

While Hadrian's Wall might be the best preserved of the *limites*, there were others. Similar defensive walls, either in stone or in wood, and earthworks were erected along the borders of Raetia and Germania, the Arabian Peninsula (province of Arabia) and the province of Dacia. In most other areas, the *limes* consisted of a line of forts, with or without a rampart with palisade and ditch. While this shows that in some areas the Romans encountered more trouble with the indigenous population than elsewhere, it also suggests that the walls functioned as ideological statements of dominance, and were not necessarily absolute borders. Even though a very late (and rather unreliable) Latin text mentions that Hadrian was 'the first to build a wall which separated the Romans from the barbarians' (*SHA, Hadrian* 11.2), through archaeological finds we can see that trade and exchange were plentiful across these borders, especially between the 'barbarians' of what is now Denmark and northern Germany, and the more south-westerly Roman provinces of Lower and Upper Germania.

Below: Locally carved fragment of a column imitating marble examples found in Italy. London, mid-1st–4th century AD. Stone, H. (with base) 25 cm, W. (with base) 33.5 cm.

Opposite: Aerial photo of the limes *in Germany, the outline of which is preserved in the modern landscape. Originally, it would have looked as depicted in the image above.*

Above: A reconstruction of part of the limes *in Germany, with wooden watchtower and palisade.*

In areas outside of the empire, Roman objects enjoyed high status related to their rarity and the difficulty of importing them. Archaeologists are unsure about the exact extent of influence the Roman Empire exerted over peripheral lands: in 2012, Roman glass beads were found for the very first time as far away as Japan, in a tomb from the fifth century AD, at which time the beads themselves were already between 100 and 400 years old. It is difficult today to reconstruct the journey these beads must have taken to reach that remote island, but their survival is evidence of their elevated and highly desired status.

CHAPTER 2
FACES OF CONQUEST

COINS FORM an incredibly useful aid for understanding the past. From their abbreviated inscriptions and their particular imagery, we can often determine precisely where certain coin types were produced. Particular cities within the empire minted their own coins, although all production was under strict imperial control, and their distribution across the empire tells us a great deal about how far people travelled and the areas over which trade took place. For example, a hoard of more than 15,000 gold and silver coins discovered in Hoxne, England, contained those that had been minted in Rome, Trier, Thessalonica and as far away as Antioch. All had made their way in the hands and purses of travellers, merchants, soldiers and government officials to East Anglia, where they were buried together.

Coins are also crucial as they allow us to deduce the dates for various archaeological discoveries. Like modern coinage and unlike some other ancient monetary systems, Roman coins are often closely dated, inasmuch as they record who was the emperor, what titles he currently held (sometimes indicating which year of his reign it was) and occasionally monumental historical events that are documented in literary sources. When these coins were dropped and lost they help to provide a date of some use for any associated archaeological discoveries. However, many of us still carry around and use coins that were struck in the 1970s, so to lose a coin minted in 1971 today does not necessarily mean that the drain or gutter it falls down was in existence back then. The coin merely indicates that whatever it was found in must have existed at some point in time *after* the coin was struck. A deposit on top of the coin, for example a floor or road surface laid over it, must therefore also have been made after the date on the coin, though how long after is impossible to know without other forms of evidence. Therefore, while coins offer a valuable starting point, they do not always, in themselves, allow firm historic dates to be known. Roman coins often remained in circulation for even longer periods of time than coins do today, sometimes for centuries. This becomes clear from the hoards of coins which are often discovered predominantly in the north-western provinces of the empire. A hoard from Bath in Britain contained coins from as early as 31 BC right up to those of the emperor Aurelian (AD 270–275), meaning that those late Republican coins had been in use for approximately 300 years before finally being taken out of circulation. So as well as helping archaeologists to date sites and finds, coins also have the potential to produce some very misleading dates.

Such a uniform monetary system was one of the key ways in which the Roman Empire established and held control. It allowed trade to flourish, taxes to be collected easily and payments made to soldiers to be spent in the areas they were stationed. In addition to these practical, economic benefits it also had a crucial role in sending information from Rome to the provinces as a tool of communication and propaganda. In the Roman Empire, a world with none of the mechanisms of communication on which we rely today, key information still needed to be shared with those living within its confines as quickly as possible; information such as news of great victories, the wealth, might and prosperity of the empire, and even changes of emperor. As mentioned earlier, the army was very effective in spreading the Roman way of life, but it was also particularly useful for communicating news. The *cursus publicus* (a state run system of couriers and relay points) allowed individual messages to be carried efficiently throughout the empire. For the vast majority of the population, however, key information needed to be available and visible in a simple and effective manner. What better way to display these messages than on every coin used for every transaction?

Despite their small size and the limited space for images and text on coins, the Romans ensured that they conveyed the maximum possible information. Just a few letters on a gold coin of the emperor Trajan (p. 44) summarized much information about him: his full name, *Imperator* (Commander) Trajan Augustus (IMP TRAIANO AVG);

honorary titles after victories over the Germanic tribes and the Dacians, *Germanicus Dacicus* (GER DAC); that he was the chief priest of Roman state religion, *Pontifex Maximus* (PM); that he held power as tribune of the people, *Tribunicia Potestas* (TRP); that he was in his fifth consulship (COS V); that he was the 'father of his country', *Pater Patriae* (PP); and that he received his powers from the Senate and the Roman people and thus was their representative, *Senatus Populusque Romanus Optimo Principi*, literally 'the Senate and the Roman people, to the best of first-citizens' (SPQR OPTIMO PRINC). All of this is recorded in an abbreviated system still echoed by the inscriptions on modern British coins.

However, since much of the population of the empire is likely to have been illiterate or at least speakers of languages other than Latin, images were arguably more important than words for communicating news and events. The image of the emperor or members of his family – a constant and fixed presence on the obverse of all Roman coins – and other depictions on the reverse which will be examined below, were designed to reinforce messages of power and status. Those messages naturally were decreed, as they are today, by those in control of the mint, the emperors themselves,

Above: Gold aureus. The obverse shows the emperor Trajan with a series of abbreviated titles. The reverse shows further titles and depicts Arabia standing holding cinnamon sticks. Rome, AD 103–11. Gold, Diam. 2 cm.

Opposite top: Gold aureus. On the reverse the emperor Titus stands over a seated Judaea. Rome, AD 72–3. Gold, Diam. 2 cm.

Opposite: Gold aureus. The emperor Domitian wears a laurel victory crown on the obverse while on the reverse Germania sits on her shield. Rome, AD 86. Gold, Diam. 2.1 cm.

and as such they tell us directly those pieces of information that the imperial house wanted everyone to know.

Conquest in all parts of the empire is a recurring theme for depictions on coinage. For example, after AD 71 coins were minted to mark the subjugation of Judaea by Titus, son of the emperor Vespasian, showing the head of Titus on the obverse and himself again standing on the reverse, spear in hand, a foot on his helmet, with Judaea, personified as a woman (as provinces usually were), seated beneath. The personification of a territory or province is a common motif, on both coins and other forms of art, and was also employed by Titus' brother, Domitian, when claiming victory over Germania in AD 86 (below). Germania is shown as a woman seated on her shield, with a broken spear and her head bowed. The level of Domitian's success in this campaign was perhaps not as great as his coinage alone would lead us to believe, but the truth was not what was required. Instead, Domitian used his coin to promote

his image as all powerful and successful conqueror, and this is what the peoples of the empire would have seen. In some cases the images on coins are also reflected in great monuments in Rome. There are a number of 'Dacia Victa' coin types which, as observed in other examples, show a female personification of the province. Dacia is forlorn and subdued in this series of coins, which tells part of the story of Trajan's conquests in Dacia, the same story that is spectacularly told on Trajan's Column.

The provinces of the empire did not only feature on coinage with direct messages of subjugated territories. Images of peaceful, prosperous territories are also shown. For example, Arabia is shown standing, holding branches and cinnamon sticks with a camel behind her (p. 44), and the personification of Egypt (below) with a lotus flower on her head, reclines gracefully, with a snake and ibis also in the scene. Rather than power by conquest and war, these images

Left: Copper sestertius. *Dacia is shown subjugated on the reverse. Rome, AD 104–11. Copper alloy, Diam. 3.4 cm.*

Below: Gold aureus. *On the reverse, Egypt (Aegyptos) is shown reclining. Rome, AD 134–8. Gold, Diam. 2 cm.*

Opposite: One of the reliefs from the Sebasteion at Aphrodisias, modern Turkey, shows the emperor Claudius forcefully subduing the province of Britannia, represented as a barbarian woman. AD 40–60. Marble, H. 165 cm, W. 135 cm.

convey the power of prosperity, abundance and wealth and, particularly in the case of Egypt, the individual wealth and might of the emperor, as Egypt was controlled directly by the emperor himself who employed its bountiful grain supply to feed the people of the city of Rome.

It should come as no surprise to see a personified Britannia featuring on Roman coins, as she later did continuously on modern British coins from 1672 to 2008. She appears in many guises during the Roman occupation from the time of Hadrian, who visited the province in AD 122 and ordered the construction of the wall (which for us bears his name) at the northernmost point of the empire at that time. She is shown literally trampled underfoot by the emperor Geta in AD 211, while in around AD 287 she greets the rebel Carausius in a welcoming manner (above). Thus Carausius used the empire's own propaganda technique to legitimize himself as an emperor. He had been commander of the Roman fleet in the north, but rebelled and made himself emperor in Britain. Unusually, his coins reference Latin authors with a legend derived from Virgil's *Aeneid* meaning 'come, long-awaited one' to accompany the image, associating himself with the foundation of Rome. Just a few years later Britannia is represented again risen from her knees and welcomed back into the empire by the emperor Constantius (opposite), a sign of forgiveness for all to see after the period of rebel rule by Carausius and his successor Allectus was ended.

Roman coinage did not just circulate within the empire but has been discovered beyond its frontiers in regions that were never subject to Roman rule. As well as being instruments of imperial propaganda they were, unlike the nominal coinage of today, intrinsically valuable objects of precious metal. A gold *aureus* of the emperor Claudius found far beyond the empire in India has a vertical chisel-cut mark on the emperor's head, possibly carried out to test the quality of the metal. The mark has been made in the thickest part of the coin with no regard for the fact that it has damaged the image of the emperor. This is quite common on Roman gold coins found in India but not within the empire, where the emperor's image was usually treated with greater respect. Coins found in these far-flung locations have been traded far outside the Roman world and, unlike the examples above, the images and messages on the coin itself are secondary to the material value of the metal from which the coin is made. Roman coins may have reached far beyond the boundaries of the empire, but their messages and ideologies appear to have had little relevance to those who then traded with them.

A different yet equally fascinating example of the spread of coins outside of the known Roman world comes from Iron Age Britain, before Claudius' conquest in AD 43 and its inclusion in the empire. Verica of the Atrebates tribe in southern Britain was recognized by Rome as a client, allied king. One of his gold coins (p. 51, left) shows a mounted horseman raising a spear, and names him REX (king) and COM F (*Commii filius*, son of Commios). Importantly, we see here a non-Roman leader using the Latin language, a title bestowed upon him by Rome and similar abbreviated forms to those used on Roman coins.

Furthermore, the image of the horseman is clearly based on an earlier Roman silver *denarius* of 82 BC, which bore the same design of a horseman with a spear (p. 51, right). The aim was to produce a coin that was clearly recognizable as having been based on Roman styles, even if the imagery and the text were not well understood by the people who used or even made them. On another coin (right) minted by Verica with the same legend, VERICA REX, the name Verica has been reversed mistakenly, probably due to a lack of understanding of the Latin alphabet by those cutting the dies. Although the skills to produce the coins may still have been being learnt, through language, title and imagery, and even by minting coins in the first place, Verica connects himself firmly with the powerful empire across the sea and thus ensures that everyone who sees and uses those coins knows his position and, perhaps more importantly, who his friends are.

Above: Silver coin with a butting bull and VERICA REX (King Verica) on the reverse. England, AD 10–40. Silver, Diam. 1.3 cm.

As demonstrated by the Verica coins, there is plenty of archaeological evidence for trading and diplomatic contact between Britain and Gaul and the wider empire in the time between Caesar and Claudius. However, the conquest of Britain was a deeply significant achievement; something that even Julius Caesar had failed to achieve. This was particularly important for Claudius, whose reputation up to the time of his becoming emperor was as a minor and weak member of the imperial family. The Claudian victory coins show a triumphal arch on the reverse on the top of which is Claudius himself on horseback with weapons collected as trophies either side. The lettering proudly declares DE BRITANN, '[a triumph] over the Britons'. The arch itself was built in Rome and a fragment of the inscription can still be seen in the Capitoline Museum there. A more obvious and distinct representation of Roman conquest and power would be hard to imagine.

Above: Gold stater *naming Verica, son of Commios, as REX (king). England, AD 10–40. Gold, Diam. 1.75 cm.*

Above right: Silver denarius. *The horseman brandishing a spear on the reverse is very similar to that on the British* stater. *Rome, 82 BC. Silver, Diam. 2.3 cm.*

We know very little first-hand about the peoples whom the Romans encountered and conquered as their empire expanded. The tribal communities of Gaul, Germany, Britain, Spain, the Balkans and western North Africa rarely practised figural art before the Roman conquest and the few surviving examples depict divinities rather than mortals. Therefore, we have almost no knowledge of how these peoples viewed themselves: they are only ever seen through Roman eyes. Surviving texts were also invariably written by Romans for a Roman audience and so we cannot know how reliable such descriptions of foreign peoples were.

The archaeological imprints of their cultures have been more useful in illuminating pre-Roman life in regions which later became subsumed into the empire. We know that in Gaul and Britain, Iron Age populations were organized into tribal groups with recognizably town-like settlements and agricultural networks. The jewellery and weapons that they buried or lost give us an idea of self-adornment and social responsibilities. They also had complex social hierarchies and religious institutions, and often their own armies, weapons and military tactics. Indeed, the Roman army constantly had to adapt its approach to war to match the strategies of its enemies, and it was this flexibility, combined with a determined refusal to accept or admit defeat that ensured its ultimate success.

The huge curved sword of the Dacians, known as the *falx*, easily sliced through the characteristic Roman body armour made of numerous strips and plates of iron (*lorica segmentata*), splitting shields and severing whole limbs with a single blow. The horrific injuries sustained by Roman soldiers during the Dacian wars were described in detail by Marcus Cornelius Fronto. The Romans were forced to retreat, but rather than admit defeat they designed new armour specifically to counter a blow from a *falx* and attacked once more, this time to greater success. For the Romans, defeat was seen as temporary – they would withdraw, reassess their tactics and come back stronger and better adapted to win. When three Roman legions led by Varus were massacred by Germanic tribes led by the local prince Arminius in the forest at Teutoburg in AD 9, it was only five years before the Romans marched again on the area. This was essentially a revenge mission to restore Roman pride since the Germanic tribes had captured the legionary standards – a great source of shame for the army and the emperor. After the eventual defeat of Arminius and the recovery of the standards, Tiberius recalled his general (confusingly named Germanicus for his previous victories over the Germans) to Rome and withdrew troops from the land beyond the Rhine, not wishing to retain this territory within the empire.

The Roman opinion of their barbarian foes, particularly the Celtic peoples of north-western Europe, written about in contemporary literature initially seems contradictory: by some authors they were portrayed as uncouth, untamed savages in dire need of the civilizing lessons of Rome; at other times they were noble, simple people with a brave spirit, unhampered by the complex pressures of Roman life and the softening of character that came through luxury and comfort. As Caesar wrote in his *Gallic Wars*: 'Of all of these tribes, the Belgae are the bravest, because they are the furthest removed from the civilization and elegance of the

Opposite: Bronze eagle found at the Romano-British town of Calleva (modern Silchester). Despite being the inspiration for Rosemary Sutcliff's book The Eagle of the Ninth, *it was probably not part of a military standard but rather may have come from a statue of Jupiter. Silchester, early 1st century AD. Bronze, H. 15 cm, L. 23 cm.*

Province [Gallia Narbonensis], and because merchants visit them least often to import those things that effeminate the mind' (Caesar, *Gallic Wars* 1.1). However, despite seeming incompatible, the two opinions worked in tandem: the barbarian way of life was not to be praised or emulated, but victory over an unworthy foe was not much to celebrate. Therefore, the bravery and fighting spirit of the barbarians was to be applauded and mentioned at every opportunity as a tool for increasing Roman pride as their conquerors.

Attitudes towards the peoples of the Hellenic and Persian worlds generally differed from feelings about those of the Celtic provinces. The Greeks were greatly admired by the Romans for their intellectual accomplishments, not to mention their art which the Roman elite imported and imitated with relish. However, they were generally seen as somewhat 'soft' – lacking the hard-nosed political acumen and military prowess on which the Romans prided themselves. To be seen as too much of a 'philhellene' (a lover of Greek culture) was, for a Roman, a sign of a weak and soft character and an accusation often levelled at the emperor Hadrian who spent a great part of his reign in the Hellenic provinces and earned the nickname *Graeculus* (Little Greek). Further east, Arabia held a particular fascination for Rome as the source of luxury goods such as spices and silks. For example, a beautiful bust shows a Persian woman wrapped tightly in a veil and wearing the distinctive curved Phrygian cap which characterized eastern people in Greek and Roman art. The immediately alien aspect of this figure demonstrates the hold that the east had on the imaginations of the people of Rome. However, she is carved in a classical style and her facial features appear European. The idealizing of foreigners expressed by this sculpture is also seen clearly in Roman images of Gallic and German foes and their actual resemblance to the people of these areas is highly doubtful.

From the Antonine dynasty onwards (mid-second century AD), many emperors themselves were of foreign origin. Trajan, and most likely also Hadrian, originated from Hispania, Septimius Severus hailed from Leptis Magna in the province of Africa Proconsularis (modern Libya) and successive Severan emperors Elagabalus and Alexander Severus came from Syria and Lebanon respectively. However, the tendency to portray foreigners in art as more amenable to Roman tastes extended to the reinvention of the people themselves and even as late as the third century AD there remained a discernible attitude of Roman cultural superiority. In a panegyric to the North African knight Septimius Severus, likely to have been grandfather to the later emperor, the poet Statius praises him thus: 'Not Punic in speech, nor in your dress, your mind is not foreign: you are Italian, Italian!' (Statius, *Silvae* 4.5). As with the Persian woman and the captive Gaul (p. 58), Severus himself was shaped into a classical 'Roman'.

Like the images on coins, Roman art throughout the empire is filled with depictions of bound captives, or of Roman soldiers and emperors crushing foreign enemies physically under their feet or their horses' hooves. It was one thing to set up such images at home in Rome where, as with the arch of Claudius and Trajan's Column, they fed an already inflated sense of cultural and moral superiority, but they also repeatedly appear in the conquered provinces themselves, visible to the very people they pertain to represent, broken and subdued. The town gates at Glanum (modern Bouches-du-Rhône in France), constructed just after Caesar's conquest around 40 BC, show images of bound and captive Gauls, as does the triumphal arch set up in another Romano-Gallic town, Carpentoracte, which was built in the first century AD. In a similar manner, the monument at Adamklissi celebrating Trajan's defeat over the Dacians was constructed in the very territory the Dacian tribes had formerly controlled (now Romania). Even in Egypt, one of the more peaceful provinces, this same aggressive visual culture is found on monuments, for example the colossal statue showing a barbarian captive (back cover). In Aphrodisias, in modern Turkey, two brothers erected a monumental temple complex for the cult of the Roman emperor with depictions of all the nations that the Romans had conquered, as well as images of the emperors physically trampling their subjects. Here, some of the monumental carved marble scenes mirror the images encountered on coins: personifications of provinces are forcefully subdued (p. 47) or captives are bound and displayed as war trophies, always with the triumphant emperor standing by and often being crowned by the winged goddess Victory (p. 60). Such a monument

Opposite: This monumental marble head of a barbarian woman is thought to be a representation of the province of Germania. A sculpture of this size and quality would possibly have been set up in a conspicuous place by the emperor, for example in one of the official imperial squares (fora) in Rome. Provenance unknown, early 2nd century AD. Marble, H. 76.5 cm.

1770

was obviously designed primarily as flattery for the ruling emperor Nero and his dynasty, but it shows conquest was not only used by emperors as expressions of their power; it could also be employed sycophantically by their subjects, in this case the local nobility, as a means of ingratiating themselves in the eyes of the emperor, showing loyalty to their new ruler and, hopefully, as a route to promotion up the ranks.

It is interesting to wonder how the native peoples of these areas responded to having such graphic reminders of their suppression erected right on their doorsteps. Would these peoples have identified with the depictions of 'barbarians' that adorned these monuments, or did their exaggerated, caricatured features make them as alien to them as they were to the Romans? The relationship between Rome and the peoples whom it conquered was far more complex than simply winner and loser. Even Rome's vast army was not large enough to suppress an empire full of hostile and volatile subjects. Lasting peace required integration of conquered people into the empire rather than abject subjugation. Tacitus tells us about the process of conquest in Britain which, following the initial military victories, employed a system of indoctrination of local elites into the Roman way of life with personal benefits for local leaders if they cooperated with Roman terms of conquest. Furthermore, as we will discuss in more detail below, conquered armies were not eradicated but subsumed into the Roman army to use their skills for, rather than against, Rome.

While attitudes towards foreigners in their native lands varied considerably, the issue of how to accommodate these foreigners within Rome itself when they were brought back as slaves was another matter altogether. Much of Rome's western territorial expansion occurred before the imperial age, most famously in the Gallic wars of Julius Caesar. It was predominantly these wars that brought swathes of foreign captives back to Rome to be sold as slaves, along with Titus' victories in Judaea towards the end of the first century AD, which saw multitudes of Jews enslaved in Roman households.

Opposite: Another relief from the Sebasteion at Aphrodisias shows the emperor Augustus accompanied by an eagle representing the Roman Empire, and by a female personification of Victory. Together they are crowning a monument of the spoils of war, with a bound captive underneath, celebrating the successful conquests of other peoples. Aphrodisias, AD 40–60. Marble, H. 159 cm, W. 159 cm.

Above: Miniature figurines of bound and seated captives. Several examples of these have been found. The holes through the side and sometimes the top of the head imply that they were used as fasteners. Britain, probably 2nd–4th century AD. Copper alloy, H. (max) 4.25 cm, W. (max) 3.2 cm.

Seneca (De Clementia 1.24.1), the philosopher and advisor to the emperor Nero, records an earlier proposal put to the Senate that slaves should be made to wear different dress to the free-born in order to easily distinguish between them. This was rapidly dropped when the danger of allowing the slave population to become aware of its size and possibly get ideas about rebellion was realized. Such an admission reveals much about the sheer number of foreigners arriving in Rome as a result of martial campaigns. Tacitus, writing around the turn of the first century AD, was particularly alarmed by the scale of immigration stating: 'Our ancestors were suspicious of the dispositions of their slaves, even when these were born in their own farms or homes and instantly received their masters' affection and care. Now we have in our households entire nations, whose customs are different and religions are foreign, or even non-existent.' (Annals 14.44). The images of subjected barbarians which adorned every corner of Rome therefore may have served a purpose other than to inflate Roman pride: they also reminded these foreigners of why they were there and who was in charge.

61

PART II:
PEOPLE
OF THE
EMPIRE

**'ONE MIGHT RIGHTFULLY SAY
THAT THE PEOPLE WHO CREATED THE
ROMAN EMPIRE ARE GREATER THAN
THE EMPIRE ITSELF.'**

JOSEPHUS, *THE JEWISH WAR* 3.5.7 (=3.107) (TRANS. SHELDON)

CHAPTER 1
FIGHTING FOR ROME

ONE OF THE ELEMENTS of the Roman Empire about which we know the most is the army. Archaeological evidence and historical sources reveal information about tactics, weapons, armour, ranks and structure, conquests, battles and even the occasional dramatic defeat. The evidence for the Roman military is also rich in the actions and personalities of individual soldiers or officers. From inscriptions and archaeological finds we can reveal a little of what life was like both for those in the army and for those who were affected by their presence.

The military was mostly shaped into the form that is most recognizable to us today by Augustus as part of the reforms he carried out on becoming Rome's first emperor. He created a long-term career force of twenty-eight legions, settling those from the disbanded legions into new colonies. Length of service in the army was increased to make a standard term of twenty-five years; soldiers were prohibited from marrying (although this was often ignored); a discharge bonus was introduced; and, crucially, non-citizen subjects of the empire were drawn in to form *auxilia* (auxiliary or support) forces. Tacitus tells us that by AD 23 there were 'cavalry divisions and auxiliary cohorts, not much inferior in strength to the legions' (*Annals* 4.5). As the empire expanded and wars were fought on many different fronts, the legionaries and auxiliaries travelled far beyond their homelands and took both the standardized systems of Roman warfare and their own specialist martial customs with them. It was normal practice to move the legions to areas away from home as a policy both to discourage rebellion and to unify the empire.

Often, especially in provinces like Germania and Britannia where frontiers were permanently garrisoned, the presence of the army had a radical effect on local culture and acted as a prominent and overt reminder of a province's new subject status. Military presence in a province was not only felt through the establishment of forts: it changed the whole shape of the landscape as well as determining the development of

Above: The eagle was a symbol of Roman military power and each legion had its own eagle standard or aquila. *This small statuette was found in Colchester. Mid-1st–4th century AD. Bronze, L. 9.7 cm, H. 8 cm.*

civilian settlement. On a large scale, roads were constructed to allow ease of military movement and towns grew up to service the needs of the army which then sometimes remained when the troops moved on. In other cases the site of a vacated army base might become a civilian settlement. Ammaedara in the province of Africa (now Haidra, Tunisia), is an example of a town that developed in this way. A fort of the *Legio III Augusta* (Third Legion) was established there, and when the legion moved on in around AD 75, a town was founded on the fort site: the imposingly entitled Colonia Flavia Augusta Aemerita Ammaedara (*CIL VIII*, 308).

Less tangibly, but equally as important, the Latin language was spread as much (if not more so) by the army as by trade or by deliberate imperial policies such as that implemented by the governor of Britain, Agricola. Tacitus (Agricola's son-in-law) tells us that Agricola 'taught the sons of the tribal chiefs in the liberal arts' and that 'those who rejected the Latin language previously, now longed for rhetoric' (*Agricola* 21.2). However, this was not an absolute transfer from one language to another. The 'Celtic' languages, which continued to be spoken in Britain, adopted some Latin loan words indicating that they must at least have been spoken simultaneously. Similarly, some pre-Roman place names continued in use after the conquest such as Calleva (Silchester), while others acquired a Latin interpretation, such as St Albans which changed from Verlamion to Verulamium.

A distinctly practical use for learning Latin was to join the army as soldiers were required to be able to speak and read it. A veteran auxiliary would have had two decades' worth of experience of Latin literacy and numeracy, as well as many other practical skills acquired during his service. Unsurprisingly, veterans were men of standing in the communities in which they then settled, which were often the same places where they had previously served. In the first two centuries AD, legionaries were almost exclusively Roman citizens, but non-citizens could still enlist in several different branches of the army, such as the auxiliary troops, the navy and the cavalry section of the emperor's bodyguards. The most important reason for their voluntary enlistment was the promise of full citizenship on discharge after twenty-five years. Only a limited percentage of all those enlisted survived for twenty-five years, especially in such war-ridden decades as around the turn of the first century AD, but considering that in those years the auxiliary troops numbered around 200,000 at any given time, any percentage still represented a significant number. Interestingly enough, the children of the auxiliaries received Roman citizenship, although not wives (in all likelihood because officially they were not allowed to marry).

One of the earliest surviving pieces of evidence of this is an inscription on a tombstone in Gaul from the time of the emperor Tiberius in the early first century AD (*ILS* 2531). The inscription describes a veteran, originally with the Gallic name Agedillus, who served for thirty-two years as an auxiliary in a cavalry regiment, and who then appears on this tomb under his Roman name of Gaius Julius Macer, with a daughter Julia Matrona and a freedman Gaius Julius Primulus. Citizenship of an empire that had conquered your people as a reward for military service may seem incongruous to us, but it was a crucial part of the Romans' system of rewards, created to engender unity and a sense of loyalty to Rome, as well as to encourage the sense that people could rise within the hierarchy of the system rather than perpetually remain its subjects.

Apart from inscriptions on tombstones, we learn a lot about people's and units' origins and careers from the surviving military diplomas that were awarded upon discharge (overleaf). These inscribed bronzes were of crucial importance in a world without digital information, as they were the only proof a veteran had to show that he was, in fact, a full citizen; and as well as his own name, the names of seven witnesses were recorded in the text, often other members of his military unit. The diploma was presented at the 'town hall' of the area in which the veteran wished to settle, where his name would be inserted in the list of Roman citizens. For two centuries Roman citizenship was of such value that thousands of provincials enlisted for twenty-five or more years, if not for themselves, then for their children. In AD 212 however, the emperor Caracalla granted citizenship to all free inhabitants of the Roman Empire. Military diplomas thus become obsolete for auxiliary troops, yet some later examples survive for the navy and the cavalry of the emperor's guard, since those troops actually included *barbari* (people from outside the boundaries of the empire).

Once a citizen, some individuals could rise rapidly into high office in Rome. One such example is Quintus Lollius Urbicus from Castellum Tidditanorum (now Tiddis, Algeria). A Roman citizen from birth, but the third son of a landowner in a province far from Rome, an inscription in his home town describes his career, which included acting as military tribune in Mainz, legate in the province of Asia, commander of *Legio X Gemina* in Vienna and legate of the emperor Hadrian in the campaign in Judaea. In AD 135 or 136, around the time that the poet Juvenal wrote complaining that the city of Rome was being polluted by an influx of easterners, Urbicus achieved one of the highest offices in Rome: consul. His career did not finish there and after his consulship Urbicus became governor, first of the whole province of Lower Germania and then of Britannia, where he oversaw the construction of the short-lived Antonine Wall. As a well-known historian remarked, at no other time but our own could a farmer from inner Africa embark on a career that took him to such exotic places, culminating in positions of the greatest power in the culture in which he lived. Yet his is not an isolated example and, as already mentioned, provincial nobility could even become emperor. We can only imagine what Juvenal would have made of that.

In a similar manner, the North African emperor Septimius Severus travelled extensively on military campaigns, fighting a successful war against the Parthian Empire and fortifying the defences along the edges of the empire in Arabia and Africa, before campaigning in the north of Britain and then finally succumbing to a fatal illness while at Eboracum (York) in AD 211. He is probably the most famous of many Romans who travelled on military campaigns to die far from their homes in distant parts of the empire. Within the collection of the British Museum are two tombstones of soldiers who died at Lincoln: Gaius Saufeius of *Legio IX* who came from Heraclea in Macedonia, and Titus Valerius Pudens of *Legio II Adiutrix* from Savaria in the province of Pannonia Superior (modern Hungary) who died at the age of thirty around AD 76.

Pudens' legion was recruited from marines of the Ravenna fleet during the Roman civil war of AD 69. The trident of the sea god Neptune between two dolphins on his tomb may refer back to the roots of the legion.

Such symbols and emblems were often used to identify units or legions, but sometimes remain a mystery to us now. Nevertheless, soldiers took enormous pride in their origins and their native fighting skills, which the Roman army was only too eager to adopt. After all, constant adaptation was needed to conquer ever-changing enemies. For example, troops from the Balearic Islands were notable slingers, Thracians professional horse riders and Syrians famous archers. One Syrian archer, Soranus, was so admired by Hadrian that it is even thought the emperor himself composed this poem for him:

I am the man, once well known to the river banks in Pannonia [eastern Europe], brave and foremost among a thousand Batavi [units from the Netherlands with whom Soranus was stationed], who, with Hadrian as judge, could swim the wide waters of the deep Danube in full battle kit. From my bow I shot an arrow which, while it hung in the air and fell back, I hit and broke with another. Whom no Roman or foreigner ever outdid, no soldier with the spear, no Parthian with the bow, here I lie, on this ever-mindful stone have I bequeathed my deeds to memory. Let anyone see if after me he can match my deeds. I set my own standard, being the first to bring off such feats.
(*CIL III*, 3676, trans. Davies, University of Edinburgh Press)

Other identifying symbols could also be integrated into the army, and one of the best known is the Draco, the standard of Dacian soldiers. The Draco was a fearsome tool of intimidation: a bronze head of a sneering wolf or dragon with several long metal tongues, and a fabric tail which fluttered behind it in the wind. It was carried on a long pole by a

Opposite: Draco from the limes *in Germany, indicating that troops of Dacian origin were stationed in this border area. Niederbieber, 3rd century AD. Bronze, L. 30 cm.*

horseman and it is said that when the wind rushed through
it, it made a horrifying shrieking sound. The Draco was the
emblem of the Dacian army and is represented several times
on Trajan's Column, carried by the Dacian enemies fighting
the Roman soldiers, as well as on coins and on a relief that
shows the spoils of war of the Dacian campaign (p. 2). After
Trajan's victory and the annexation of their territory in the

Roman Empire, however, Dacian troops were recruited into the Roman army and many were posted in Britain. They continued to carry their unique standard and it is seen on the fourth-century Arch of Galerius in Greece and on tombstones of Roman Dacian soldiers in Britain, most famously one at Chester. Its legacy is highly interesting, as one theory links the dragon on the flag of Wales with the Dacian Draco. In short, the inclusion of these native elements

Above: A scene from Trajan's Column in Rome, at the top of which Dacian warriors are shown carrying the Draco standard in battle. Once Dacians were assimilated into the Roman army, they continued to use this standard as their personal symbol.

in the Roman army shows its diversity, tolerance and even perhaps encouragement of foreigners: the Roman army was 'Roman' in the sense that it served Rome, but its make-up was a mixture of foreign, indigenous and Roman elements.

The forts along the line of Hadrian's Wall at the far north of the empire can give us a fascinating snapshot of how the Roman army moved people from their homelands to fight or garrison in other areas. There were physical barriers elsewhere in the empire, including Germania where Hadrian ordered a palisade to be built marking the line of the frontier between the Rhine and Danube, but Hadrian's Wall is the frontier most familiar to us today, despite there being barely any reference to it in the historical record. As mentioned previously, Hadrian's Wall seems to have acted as a way of controlling passage between the empire and the land beyond rather than entirely preventing it. Either way, there was a large force at and near the wall and studies have revealed that more than forty different auxiliary units were based there during its history. Auxiliary units have ethnic titles which don't necessarily reflect the ethnicity of all of their members, but instead refer to where the unit was formed. However, by looking at the diversity of these units we can get an indication of the extent to which the military moved people across the empire.

The only known native British unit to have been stationed on the wall was the *Cohors I Cornoviorum*, which was recruited from the tribe centred at what is now Wroxeter in Shropshire. There were large numbers of units from modern Germany, France and Belgium and some also from the Netherlands, Switzerland, Romania, Bulgaria and Hungary. Amongst those who were furthest from their place of formation was the *Cohors I Hamiorum Sagittariorum* from Syria, who, as archers, may have had the added function of supplying meat and game to the troops. In addition, the *Numerus Maurorum Aurelianorum*, the soldiers of the emperor Aurelian's Moorish unit from North Africa, based at the fort of Aballava (Burgh-by-Sands) at the western end

This statue of bronze
representing Hercules was found
on an estate of Lord Carlisle's and Duc
on the Roman Wall in Cumberland

GIVEN BY
A WOLLASTON FRANKS, K.C.B
1895.

of the wall, were perhaps as far from home as was possible without leaving the empire's territories.

Arbeia (South Shields) was the easternmost point at which troops were stationed for the wall, guarding a small seaport on the south bank of the Tyne estuary. This fort gives an indication of how changes in troop deployment happened over time. Arbeia seems to have been built originally during the reign of Hadrian, around AD 129, by the *Legio VI Victrix Pia Fidelis*. The first unit to be stationed there was a cavalry squadron recruited from the Pannonian tribes of modern Hungary. This was followed by a cavalry regiment from north-west Spain. The cavalry units were replaced in the time of Septimius Severus by *Cohors V Gallorum*, a thousand-strong Gallic infantry unit and finally, and perhaps most interestingly, the last unit that we know of was the *Numerus Barcariorum Tigrisiensium*, a unit of barge-men from the river Tigris in what is now Iraq. The name of this unit is listed in the *Notitia Dignitatum*, an official list of all civil and military posts dated to around AD 400, just before the Romans officially withdrew from Britain, and it is believed to be the reason why the fort bears the name Arbeia, perhaps meaning 'place of the Arabs'.

Amongst the evidence of these different units at Arbeia are some intriguing stories of individuals who accompanied the military. A tombstone inscription (*RIB* 1064) commemorates Victor, aged 20, 'of the Moorish nation', a freedman of Numerianus of the Spanish cavalry we noted above, who dedicates the memorial 'most devotedly'. Victor, having begun his life in Africa, lived first as a slave to and then freeman of a Spanish master, only to die at a very young age in the northernmost point of the empire. Displayed alongside Victor's tombstone at the museum at Arbeia is the tombstone of Regina, one of the few indigenous Britons who can be firmly identified in the archaeological record. Her tombstone was found outside the civilian settlement which grew up around Arbeia. The exact spot is marked today by a replica tomb in a supermarket car park in South Shields.

Regina and her tomb are almost perfect examples of the
melting pot that was Roman Britain and the Roman Empire
as a whole. The tomb dates to the late second century, the
time when the emperor Septimius Severus was launching
campaigns into Scotland as well as commissioning major
building works at both Arbeia and Coria (Corbridge).

The manner in which Regina is depicted is an interesting
story in its own right and is recounted in more detail later
in the book. However, the inscriptions below her are of
interest here. There are two, the first in Latin, in a standard
format, which translates as 'To the spirits of the departed
[and] to Regina, his freedwoman and wife, a Catuvellaunian,
aged thirty, Barates of Palmyra [set this up]'. So Regina
was born as a member of the Catuvellauni, a tribe based
around Verulamium (St Albans), which was a *municipium*
(municipality), whose magistrates became Roman citizens.
At some point she became a slave to Barates, who later
freed her and married her. Barates himself has an equally
interesting story. In the Latin inscription he states he is
Barates of Palmyra, which was in the Roman province of
Syria, and held a position of importance as a point on the
trade route linking the empire with India and the east.
Hadrian visited Palmyra in AD 129, the very year that
Arbeia was most likely constructed, and was so taken with
it that he renamed it Palmyra Hadriana. Beneath the Latin
inscription is another in the Palmyrene script, a dialect of
Aramaic, which reads 'Regina, the freedwoman of Barates,
alas'. The sculptor seems to be more at home with the
cursive Palmyrene than with the Latin (which contains some
grammatical errors), perhaps indicating that he was himself
from the east of the empire.

A tombstone for a Barates who may have been Regina's
husband has also been discovered around 30 kilometres
away at Corbridge. His tombstone is of much poorer quality
and reads, in Latin only, 'To the spirits of the departed,
Barates of Palmyra, *vexillarius*, lived sixty-eight years'. If
the same man, Barates must have stayed in the north of

PART II: PEOPLE

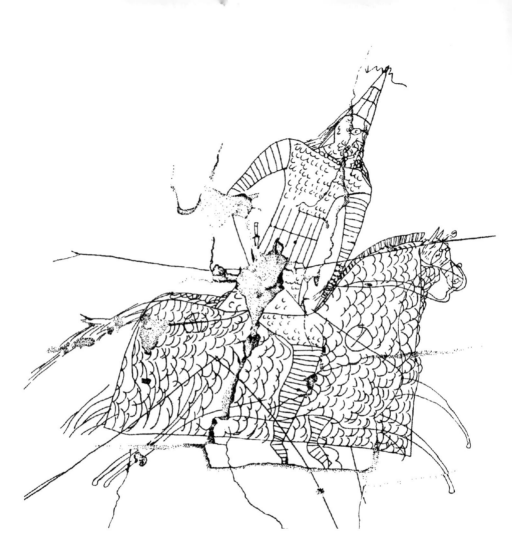

Britain after the death of Regina, although his fortune seems to have declined considerably, or perhaps his heirs were less inclined to spend money on his memorial than he had been for Regina. There is debate about the term *vexillarius*: usually this would mean a standard bearer in the military, but Barates is far too old still to be serving. He may have settled near to where he had previously been stationed as so many retiring soldiers did. Alternatively he may have been a trader supplying standards to the army. There is much that these stones cannot tell us, but they are a fascinating window into

Above: Graffiti from Dura Europos known as the 'charging clibanarius' dating to the mid-3rd century AD. The image shows the typical heavy armour of both horse and rider worn by eastern elite soldiers of the time. Dura Europos was sacked by the Persians in AD 255–7.

Above: Soldier's badge or baldric fastener from Nineveh, modern Iraq, 2nd–3rd century AD. Copper alloy, Diam. 6.6 cm.

an ancient world, not so unlike our own, where a man from Syria might come to Britain, marry a local woman, settle and finally die there.

It is not only within the formal boundaries of the empire that we find evidence of Roman military activity. Moving to the eastern borders, Roman material has also been found at Nineveh, now modern Iraq. Nineveh was situated in the independent state of Adiabene, in between the Parthian and Roman empires. Finds of pottery, coins and military equipment hint that there was Roman campaigning in the

Opposite: Cast
statuette of a figure
in Roman military
dress found in modern
Yemen, 1st–2nd
century AD. Copper
alloy, H. 9.1 cm,
D. 2.3 cm.

area and even that Nineveh briefly may have been part of the Roman Empire. It is likely that the Roman material was used while it was in Roman hands, but equally it may have made its way there while Nineveh was beyond the official boundaries of the Roman world.

The imagery of the Roman military travelled further than the army itself. Within the collection of the British Museum is a tiny bronze statuette of a figure in Roman military dress, depicted as a three-layered pleated skirt, which was found in Yemen. He may be an imitation of Mars, who is usually shown with a crested helmet, similar to the one this figure wears. The statuette is most likely a deity and has a dish (*patera*) in one hand; he holds his other arm aloft as if grasping a spear, which is now lost. This figure from the Middle East bears many similarities to examples from Roman Britain, which mix British and Roman attributes in the same way as the Nineveh figure combines eastern and Roman influences; and we have already seen Horus from Roman Egypt resplendent in Roman armour in a different blending of Roman and eastern images (p. 11). So we can see that the Roman army had a profound impact across the conquered provinces – not just in terms of the development of civilian settlements and new frontiers, but also on the cultures of these lands, with the merging of local and Roman imagery on artworks and the spread of the Latin language.

CHAPTER 2
TRADING FOR 'PEACE'

So many ships arrive here with all that is needed on board, from everywhere, during any season, and after every harvest. The city looks like the collective market for the entire world. You can marvel at large cargoes from India, or if you wish, at those from Arabia … Clothing from Babylonia and decorations from foreign lands beyond come into Rome more easily than those from Naxos or Kythnos reach Athens … Egypt, Sicily and Libya are now your farms. Ships never cease to come and go.

(Aelius Aristides, *Orationes 26: In Praise of Rome*)

SO WROTE Aelius Aristides in AD 155 in a piece entitled *In Praise of Rome*. Aristides is not likely to be exaggerating. Additional evidence from legal documents detailing how transactions were carried out, as well as archaeological finds, including those from shipwrecks laden with cargo, indicate that there were large quantities of goods moving around the empire. We do not completely understand how trade was perceived by the Romans and whether they would have considered their transactions as part of an economy in the sense that we understand it today. There are likely to have been many elements of local, regional and cross-empire relationships which could be private, state or commercial exchange all happening concurrently. In order to carry out these transactions, there were certainly traders, merchants, slaves, freedmen, soldiers and sailors moving and travelling all across and beyond the empire, trading, exchanging and, consciously or otherwise, sharing their customs, habits and beliefs.

As seen earlier in the book when discussing the coins from the reign of Verica in Britain, there was certainly contact with and influence from the Roman Empire before the military conquest of Britain. Written sources confirm this: as early as 70 BC, Cicero, defending Marcus Fonteius, the ex-governor of Transalpine Gaul from a maladministration charge (which included introducing an arbitrary tax on

wine), stated that 'Gaul is crammed with merchants and filled with Roman citizens' (*For Marcus Fonteius*, 11). Twenty years later, when Julius Caesar was planning his invasion of Britain, he wrote in the *Gallic Wars* that he summoned merchants (*mercatores*) to share their knowledge of British territory 'because apart from merchants, nobody goes there without good reason' (*Gallic Wars* 4.20). Traders accompanied armies and even went in advance of them, seeing commercial opportunities beyond the official boundaries of the empire. They supplied the armies that were conquering new territories and afterwards remained to make profits from civilian populations, developing markets for Roman goods and foodstuffs amongst peoples who were literally buying into Rome.

This early contact in Britain is also demonstrated by some of the goods and objects that appear in the archaeological record. A good example is a late Iron Age burial in Welwyn in Hertfordshire. The burial was that of a high-status man whose body had been wrapped in a bear skin and then cremated, with his burnt bones placed in a pile on the floor of the burial vault. The burial dates from the period in between Julius Caesar's expeditions to Britain in 55 and 54 BC and Claudius' invasion of AD 43. The grave was filled with many pots and metal vessels, wooden bowls and buckets and even a set of gaming pieces which may have been used for a game similar to ludo. Most of the objects in the grave were native to Iron Age Britain, but there are also Roman platters, a large flagon from Gaul and a silver cup and amphorae (storage jars) from Italy. Whether or not they were traded commercially or were exchanged in some way, their presence in the grave indicates that they were exotic objects and tells us that even at that time there were people moving goods beyond the official boundaries of the empire.

Some ancient writers, as well as modern scholars, suggest that there were firm commercial and economic reasons for physically expanding the territory of the empire. The name Britannia may derive from the Phoenician name Baratanac, meaning 'land of tin'. Despite Cicero's observation at the time of Caesar's expeditions that 'I hear that in Britain there is neither gold or silver' (*Letters to Friends* 7.7), Strabo, writing in the early first century AD in the reign of the emperor Tiberius, discusses the goods that were exported from Britain saying, 'it produces grain, cattle, gold, silver and iron: all of these are taken from it, as are animal hides, slaves and dogs that are naturally suited for hunting' (*Geography* 4.5.2). Tacitus also deliberately celebrates these resources as a justification for invasion, saying 'As the price of conquest, Britain produces gold, silver and other metals' (*Agricola* 12). While Claudius needed a decisive military victory to affirm him as a strong emperor (having allegedly been reluctant to accept the imperial 'purple' following the murder of Caligula), the economic benefits to be gained

Below: Pewter dining vessels from Roman Britain. Plate: Lincolnshire, 4th century AD. Pewter, Diam. 36.4 cm. Flagon: Selsey, 4th century AD. Pewter, H. 26.3 cm.

from Britain's natural and human resources must have been another powerful motivation for invasion.

Not all trading was done on a pan-empire scale: local and regional industries could also thrive within it. Britain was certainly rich in lead and there was a general use of pewter dishes, although the very wealthy were able to purchase or import silverware. Sometimes, exchange and movement of goods happened, as today, on a very personal level rather than a commercial one, and gift giving was an important aspect in shoring up diplomatic bonds.

Vindolanda was an important auxiliary fort on the northern frontier of Britain before the building of Hadrian's Wall and excavations in 1973 uncovered writing tablets that had been preserved in the waterlogged conditions. The tablets are made of thin slices of wood, written on with quill-type pens using carbon and display a great variety of individual handwriting. These, and hundreds of other fragments that have come to light in subsequent excavations, are the oldest surviving handwritten documents in Britain. Most of the tablets are official military documents relating to the auxiliary units stationed at the fort; others, however, are private letters sent to or written by the serving soldiers. The content is fascinating, giving us a remarkable insight into the working and private lives of the Roman garrison.

Amongst the Vindolanda tablets is a letter (Tablet 346) received by one of the soldiers, which reads '... I have sent [?] you ... pairs of socks from Sattua, two pairs of sandals and two pairs of underpants, ... Greet ... Tetricus and all your messmates with whom I pray that you live in the greatest good fortune.' For a soldier stationed in northern Britain we can imagine that a parcel of socks and underpants would be very well received, and that perhaps only a mother would think of sending such a gift.

At the other end of scale, Samian ware or *terra sigillata* (pottery moulded with patterns) was one of the most commercially traded goods. The most prolifically produced of all Roman fine pottery, it was used across the empire and beyond. Although predominantly manufactured in Italy, Gaul and North Africa, there are vessels and fragments to be seen in almost every archaeological collection in the region of the Roman Empire today, even as far away as Iraq. It is easily recognizable by its orange-red colour and glossy surface and is found in a vast range of styles, some plain, some very intricately decorated in relief. It was imported in great quantities to Britain. A dedicatory inscription (*ILS* 4751) survives in the Rhineland from a Marcus Secundinius Silvanus who describes himself as a '*negotiator cretarius Britannicianus*', an official pottery merchant in the Britannia trade.

Some Samian vessels never reached the wealthy clients and dining tables they were destined for, having been

*Above: Samian
ware dish from the
shipwreck at Pudding
Pan Rock, Kent.
Puy-de-Dôme, France,
2nd century AD.
Pottery, H. 5.5 cm,
Diam. 10.3 cm.*

carried by ships which sank before they reached port. Large
numbers of such pieces have been recovered from a wreck
at Pudding Pan Rock in Herne Bay in Kent, a ship with a
cargo of Samian pottery all in plain forms, which was lost en
route from Gaul to Britain in the late second century. Roman
bowls were first found by fishermen in the eighteenth
century and to this day local fishermen still find pottery
nearby as the wreck has been dispersed over a large area.
It is said that Gustavus Brander (1720–87), a Trustee of the
British Museum, once served dessert to fellow antiquaries

PART II: PEOPLE

from dishes found at Pudding Pan Rock, so some of the pottery at least has been used for its intended purpose.

Another feature of Samian ware is that it is often stamped with a maker's mark. Name stamps on decorated vessels give the name of the producing factory, but plain dishes, such as the ones from Pudding Pan Rock, have the names of the individual makers. The dishes from Pudding Pan Rock have stamps from almost forty different potters. From these we can identify the people who actually made the vessels and how widely their work was distributed throughout the empire.

Samian pottery became so popular all over the Roman world that local imitations started to appear. British examples include tableware from the Nene Valley, strongly influenced by designs we find on imported Samian pots. These imitations were made and traded across the province of Britannia from the second to fourth centuries AD. They do not seem to have reached Gaul or beyond. However, in other crafts expertise, availability of materials and production spaces were less 'portable', and therefore it was the artisans themselves who travelled. The early geometric mosaics at Fishbourne Roman Palace in West Sussex were probably made by Italian mosaicists, as mosaics were a new introduction to Britain after the conquest and there were no native craftsmen with the expertise to create them at that time.

As tastes became more Roman, vast quantities of wine, olive oil and fish sauce were, like Samian ware, imported into Britain and other regions of the empire. Another of the Vindolanda tablets (Tablet 302) shows a shopping list with a mixture of locally available goods and imported ones '… bruised beans, two *modii*, chickens, twenty, a hundred apples, if you can find nice ones, a hundred or two hundred eggs, if they are for sale there at a fair price. … 8 *sextarii* of fish-sauce … a modius of olives'. Roman influences varied the diet of the Britons as they brought a number of vegetables into the province for the first time. These included onions, garlic, peas, cabbage, celery, radish and asparagus

as well as herbs such as rosemary, thyme, bay and basil. New farming practices were also introduced, with higher yielding grains and the cultivation of fruits including apples (perhaps explaining the concern about finding 'nice' ones in the Vindolanda shopping list), mulberries, cherries and, unsurprisingly, grapes. The best wines were vintages from Italy, such as Caecuban, Falernian and Setian, but wines were produced, traded and drunk across the empire. Wine amphorae are a common find on archaeological sites from Britain to Egypt and beyond. The Romans, like the Greeks before them, drank their wine watered down: to drink it neat was considered a sign of the upmost barbarity. Beer was also considered a drink for barbarians but was still popular with the army. Once again, the Vindolanda tablets give us personal insight through a letter from a squadron commander to his prefect (Tablet 628). At the end of his request for the clarification of his orders, he says, 'My fellow soldiers have no beer. Please order some to be sent'. Clearly these soldiers had a taste for beer, despite some others' snobbery towards it.

With such a high level of trade and financial transactions, legal and administrative practices were needed to ensure the smoothest possible operations. The writing

tablet examples from Vindolanda are of course from a
military setting in which the operational activities are
regulated by the army. However, there are lesser-known
wooden writing tablets from other parts of Roman Britain in
civilian environments. The Roman villa in the Chew Valley
in Somerset has some highly significant and in some cases
rare finds, including wood and organic remains recovered
from within a well. Amongst these are the remains of a legal
document recording transactions concerning real estate,
written in a clear, neat hand on a thin sheet of larch wood in
the third century AD.

Due to the perishable nature of paper and wood, the
detail discussed in these private documents from Roman
Britain is paralleled only by the papyri of Roman Egypt,
but through these we see that the same concerns were felt
by people at both ends of the empire. The Chew Valley
real estate tablet compares well to another legal document,
this time a papyrus from Oxyrhynchus, dated to AD 187,
a contract concerning an inheritance. In this case the
contracting parties are two women, Platonis, alias Ophelia,
and Heras. In another document from the same site is a
notice to the courts concerning a contract for a loan made to
a woman named Teteoris, acting with her son and guardian,

*Above: Wooden writing
tablet from the villa
in the Chew Valley,
Somerset, 3rd century AD.
Larch, L. 16.8 cm,
H. 5.1 cm.*

*Right: Papyrus
inheritance contract
from Oxyrhynchus,
Egypt, dating to AD 187.
The contracting parties
are both women –
Platonis, alias Ophelia,
and Heras. Papyrus,
H. 12.8 cm, W. 9 cm.*

from a Roman citizen Marcus Longinus Castresius. The
document has been crossed through at a later date, showing
that the loan has been repaid. Such pertinent human
elements connect us to the lives of these individuals living
and working in Roman Egypt, just as the Vindolanda tablets
give us an insight into personal details of life on a military
fort at the opposite end of the empire at around the same
time.

More so than Britannia, Egypt formed a crucial part
of the trading networks of the empire. Along with the
other provinces of North Africa, Egypt literally fed Rome,
providing grain for the population which the surrounding

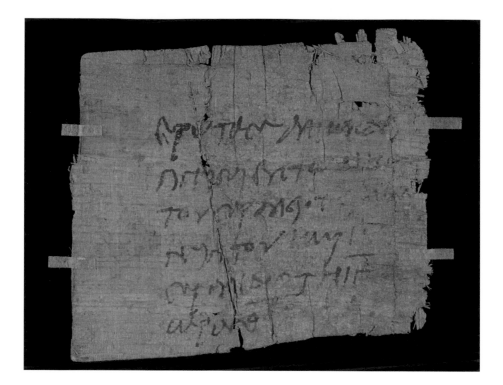

countryside could not supply. In addition, Egypt held a monopoly for the production of papyrus and traded in some of the most common coloured marbles for many of the grand building projects of Rome described earlier. Such was Egypt's importance that it had special status as an imperial province governed by a prefect from the middle class on behalf of the emperor, preventing senators having any control over it.

Egypt was also the key to the Romans' trade with India and the east. Earlier we saw that Roman coins had reached India and were valued literally for their weight in gold. The trade with the east was the reason for the presence of these coins as they were part of a trading system which brought 'exotic' products such as ivory, spices and wild beasts for the gladiatorial games into the empire. A document written in Greek in the mid-first century, known as the *Periplus of the Erythraean (Red) Sea*, describes navigation and trade routes

Above: Some surviving documents are very personal in their content. This papyrus from Oxyrhynchus, Egypt has six lines of Greek text, which contains an invitation from a man named Apion to dine 'at the table of Lord Serapis, in the dining-room of the Serapeum' on the 13th [of the month], at the ninth hour. 2nd–3rd century AD. Papyrus, H. 4.8 cm, W. 5.6 cm.

Opposite: Two-handled flask from Nineveh, modern Iraq, dating from the 2nd century AD. An identical example has been excavated from a tomb in Bahrain. Glass, H. 7.6 cm, Diam. (body) 6.8 cm.

from Roman ports including those in Egypt and Africa to the Indian subcontinent. One chapter specifically describes the goods imported and exported from India, with Roman goods including wine, copper, 'thin clothing' and 'beautiful hand maidens' for the king's harem, being exchanged for ivory, agate, carnelian, silk and peppers. This trade can be

traced archaeologically. Finds from the site of Pattanam
in south-west India include thousands of sherds of Roman
amphorae and pottery, showing that the taste for wine
and other Roman habits had spread far beyond the formal
control of the empire. Glass, that other appealing Roman
product, is also found across the empire and beyond,
including as far away as Pattanam. Trade in glass was so
pervasive that two almost identical glass bowls, one found
in Buckinghamshire, the other in Nineveh, may even have
been made in the same workshop.

Unfortunately, those Romans setting out from the
province of Egypt or any other harbour, engaging in this
trade and spreading, intentionally or otherwise, personal
Roman tastes, remain almost entirely anonymous. However,
in addition to the people mentioned in the Vindolanda tablets
and the legal papyri of Egypt, we get another tantalizing
glimpse of them from some inscribed graffiti in a cave at
Wadi Mineh about 80 kilometres east of Luxor. The cave
was used as a shelter for those travelling on the trade route
to India, and among the inscriptions we find the names of

*Above: Ribbed
marbled blue
glass bowl found
at Radnage,
Buckinghamshire,
but probably made
in Italy, and almost
identical to the Bahrain
example opposite.
Mid-1st century AD.*

Above: Glass ribbed bowl. This purple marbled example was found in modern Bahrain. 1st century AD. H. 4.5 cm, Diam. 13 cm.

Publius Annius Plocamus and his slave Lysa. A freedman of an Annius Plocamus is mentioned by Pliny the Elder as making the first contact with the king of what is now Sri Lanka, after having been blown off course on a voyage around Arabia (*Natural History* 6.84). The king is reported to have then sent an embassy to the emperor Claudius. It is tempting to see these two people as one and the same and conjecture that as early as the mid-first century AD, Rome's influence was being felt from Britain to the very southern tip of India.

CHAPTER 3
LOOKING 'ROMAN'

AS WE HAVE already seen, there were only a few places in the Roman Empire that had never experienced any influence from Rome prior to full annexation. Artistically, it is more accurate to think of Graeco-Roman influence since the Romans borrowed heavily from the Greeks in their art and architecture, basing their temples and some types of public building on Greek prototypes and importing Greek statues directly from the east, as well as creating their own versions of them in great numbers to adorn public spaces and the homes of the rich. Many areas of their empire had already experienced the influence of these artistic styles directly from the Greeks themselves, particularly the provinces of the Near East and parts of North Africa. Those of north-western Europe had had less direct contact, but the material remains of pre-Roman Britain and Gaul also attest to a degree of cultural influence which reached these areas before the legions did. The impact of this artistic style on local traditions, however, was greatly increased by the coming of the Romans themselves.

Above: Funerary monument for a cremation burial showing a reclining woman holding a bust of her husband. The woman's hairstyle is typical of the late 1st– early 2nd century AD and similar to that on the hairpin from Britain (opposite). Possibly from Rome, c. AD 100–110. Marble, H. 73.8 cm, L. 154 cm.

Opposite: Hairpin decorated with the bust of a woman wearing an elaborate hairpiece. London, late 1st century AD. Bone, L. 19.5 cm.

Opposite top: Pestle and mortar pendant, possibly used to grind pigments for personal adornment in both pre-Roman and Roman Britain Hockwold, 1st–2nd century AD. Copper alloy, L. (mortar) 10.6 cm; L. (pestle) 7 cm.

While changes in monumental art are relatively easy to trace, how this contact affected people's personal appearance and self-perception is harder to understand. In addition, the evidence that survives from different parts of the empire suggests varying degrees of change in different areas. In the north-western provinces, habitation altered to unrecognizable proportions, with the large-scale abandonment of hill forts and settlements of round houses (the settlement structure of the Celtic peoples) in favour of rectilinear structures organized around public spaces and buildings such as bathhouses, fora (public squares) and amphitheatres, all linked together by extensive road networks. However, in the more personal sphere, the change was less dramatic. Fashions from Rome in the realms of appearance, dining and creature comforts were adopted piecemeal and some native traditions held strong or evolved to represent hybrid practices.

By studying objects of personal adornment that have been discovered in different provinces of the empire, we can see how fashions and personal appearance changed under the influence of Roman tastes. A hairpin found in Gloucestershire is decorated with a finial in the form of a female bust sporting a dramatic hairstyle made up of row upon row of curls piled on top of her head. This hairstyle is seen on several portrait statues and funerary monuments of

female members of the imperial house or the Roman aristocracy during the Flavian period (the second half of the second century). Its presence on this Romano-British hairpin suggests that the women of the province were knowledgeable of and enthusiastic to adopt the fashions of their Mediterranean contemporaries. Moreover, the existence and production of hairpins themselves in this period – a rare object in pre-Roman Britain – demonstrates a change in styling techniques following assimilation within the empire, as the remarkable discovery of a preserved hairpiece fixed with two jet pins from a grave from York attests. Other new items of jewellery suggest cultural changes of a similar magnitude. For the first time we see the emergence of marriage rings, typically adorned with two clasped hands in a pose referred to as the *dextrarum iunctio*. These objects suggest the possibility not only of changes in self-adornment, but also in social institutions and how rites of passage were conducted.

Changes in personal appearance were also taking place on the other side of the empire. A series of beautiful naturalistic portraits on wood of individuals who lived and died in the first three centuries of Roman Egypt have been preserved by the arid conditions of the province, especially from the cemeteries of the Fayum basin. The portraits are painted according to classical

Left: Marriage ring decorated with the dextrarum iunctio, a symbol of two clasped hands. Norfolk, 2nd–3rd century AD. Gold, Diam. (outside) 2.3 cm.

Below: Mummy portrait from Hawara, Egypt, AD 140–160. The gold head ornament worn by the man suggests that he was a priest of Serapis. Wax and limewood, H. 42.5 cm, W. 22.2 cm.

Greek and Roman conventions, rather than traditional Egyptian style, and they depict people dressed in the tunics and clothes of the most fashionable classes in Rome, with elaborate hairstyles, laurel wreaths and jewellery that was popular throughout the empire. Interestingly, almost all names that accompany them are Greek, raising the possibility that these were not Roman immigrants to the region, but the descendants of the Hellenistic Kingdom of Ptolemy which ruled Egypt after the conquest of Alexander the Great. These paintings show us how the local elite wanted to be perceived for posterity – as part of the Roman world. However, this transformation was only skin deep: the portrait would be laid above the head of the deceased, who was mummified in the traditional Egyptian manner, and bound to the corpse with linen which was sometimes still decorated with two-dimensional images of Egyptian gods in traditional style. This reveals that, while physical appearance in everyday life may have altered radically, beliefs about death and the afterlife had changed less. Moreover, evidence for open mortuary structures in the cemeteries where the portraits are found suggest that the mummified bodies, adorned with their painted faces, would have been kept visible and on public display for a period of time before being buried. This juxtaposition of Roman face with Egyptian mummified body (not to mention Greek names) is testament to the melting pot of cultural identity and identity-display that characterized life in the Roman provinces.

In other cases, change was more subtle. The beautiful early Romano-British 'chatelaine brooch' (p. 108) in the British Museum's collection is an example of the incorporation of Roman habits and tastes as well as the tenacity of native style. 'Chatelaine brooches' were functional objects consisting of a series of handy utensils attached to an ornamental pin. They are known from pre-Roman Britain but are rare discoveries and seem to have been conspicuously displayed on the body as

Below: Star ornament from a diadem. This gold jewel is strikingly similar to that seen in the previous mummy portrait and was also found in Egypt, 1st–3rd century AD. Gold, Diam. 3.4 cm.

Left: Mummy portrait from Rubaiyat, Egypt, c. AD 160–70. The man is dressed in the uniform of a military officer. Wood (probably oak) and mastic, H. 43 cm, W. 16.5 cm.

Right: Burial cloth from Egypt, c. AD 190–220. The portrait is painted in a Graeco-Roman style while the background images are rendered in two-dimensional Pharaonic style showing Egyptian deities. Linen, L. 138 cm, W. 56 cm.

indicators of high social status. They are most common in the immediate pre-conquest period and their popularity was probably linked to the increased influence of Roman trade during this time, implying that the local elite was expressing its distinction from the remainder of society through exotic 'Roman' goods. The utensils suspended from the example here include several items indicative of Roman grooming habits, such as tweezers, a nail-cleaner and an ear-scoop.

However, the heavy enamel decoration is fundamentally
native British. The whole is an object reflective of changed
concepts of personal hygiene that had been influenced by
Roman customs, but displayed to convey conspicuous notions
of native heritage.

Objects which preserved native styles were worn
alongside those of new and imported tastes. Snakes featured
prominently in Graeco-Roman jewellery but such imagery is
rarely seen in pre-Roman art, at least that of north-western
Europe. Bracelets and finger rings in the form of coiled
snakes are perhaps the most recognizable and distinctive
indicators of Greek and Roman fashion and are discovered in
large numbers across the empire (overleaf). They range from
pieces of exquisite workmanship made of gold and precious
gems to the simplest of iron loops, indicating that the image
of the snake was adopted by all levels of society.

It was not only Roman customs that spread outwards
to other parts of the empire. The increased trade networks

that tied the provinces to one another, and the movement of people to places previously unknown or only vaguely familiar, brought cultural exchange in many directions. The oil flask adorned with African heads, discovered in Bayford Orchard, Kent (overleaf), is just one piece of evidence showing that peoples of African descent were known in Britain. Furthermore, in the third and fourth centuries AD, a habit of filling the coffins of the dead with white powder (either gypsum, chalk or lime) became popular among the wealthier members of Romano-British society. Although the reason for this burial rite remains unclear, it is believed to have originated in North Africa since this is where the earliest examples have been noted. These customs are likely to have been brought to different parts of the empire directly by foreigners themselves, rather than relayed by the army or merchants. Combined with the evidence from tombstones mentioned earlier, new techniques of forensic analysis using the skeletons of the dead from the Roman period are revealing evidence for the ethnic background of the people

Above: Bracelet in the form of a snake, from a hoard of Roman jewellery and coins found at Snettisham, Norfolk. 2nd century AD. Silver, L. 18.7 cm, W. 2.1 cm.

who lived and died in the towns of Roman Britain. The most famous is the 'ivory bangle lady' from York, a woman buried with exotic and expensive grave goods of ivory bracelets, glass vessels and objects suggestive of Christian belief. Recent analysis of her remains suggests that she was of North African descent. Other individuals from Dorset have been identified as Greek and the results of a major research project at the University of Reading reveal that up to 30 per cent of individuals buried in the large urban cemeteries of Britain were not native to the area.

This new understanding of 'civilian' migration through burial evidence leads us to consider the role that death had on the expression of personal identity. On the one hand, burial rituals are culturally specific and deviations from them attract attention and often suspicion. On the other, for all but the rich and famous, they are personal events

Below: Twisted bracelet with snake heads and a sardonyx gem, said to be from Egypt, 3rd century AD. Gold and sardonyx, Diam. 6.7 cm.

for close associates of the deceased and are receptive to idiosyncratic modification. Archaeological evidence for funerary rituals is of predominantly two types. Firstly, there are the human remains themselves. Secondly, there are the crafted goods deposited with, or for the sake of, the dead. In the late nineteenth and early twentieth centuries, it was considered that, apart from crude assessments of ethnicity linked to the size and shape of the skull (a practice largely rejected today), only the second form of evidence could be used to answer questions of cultural or ethnic identity. Much scholarship at this time was devoted to connecting various forms of grave goods to different geographical regions and, by extension, the people with whom they were found in graves. However, recent forensic techniques which analyse teeth can trace evidence for the part of the world in which

Above: Oil flask decorated with African heads from Bayford, Kent, 2nd century AD. Bronze, H. 5.4 cm.

Opposite top: Burial chest of Titus Valerius Secundus, soldier in the Seventh Praetorian Cohort. Ephesus, modern Turkey, c. AD 50–100. Marble, L. 60.95 cm, H. 41.25 cm.

Opposite below: Burial chest with a bilingual inscription in the native Greek and the official Latin. It reads in both languages: 'Pannychus (had this made) for himself, for his wife Pithane, and for his daughter Pithane'. Ephesus, modern Turkey, AD 50–100. Marble, L. 41.9 cm, H. 36.15 cm.

the deceased spent the early years of their lives. The results of this analysis are dramatically altering our perception of multiculturalism within the Roman Empire by revealing far greater evidence for migration to Britain from North Africa, the Mediterranean and even Scandinavia. This diverse ethnic makeup, however, is rarely visible in any funerary offerings that these individuals received, perhaps suggesting cultural integration and acceptance of the customs of their new home, or at least no strong desire to use foreign rites to differentiate themselves from the majority of the population. This, however, was not always the case.

As discussed earlier, cultural tensions could run high and occasionally funerary monuments – designed to last as visible reminders of the dead for centuries (as, indeed, they have) – betray overt national pride. We have already noted the tombstone of a woman named Regina, who died at the age of 30 in northern Britain. Her tombstone is one such monument. This is one of the most interesting social documents to have been discovered in Roman Britain and reveals much about the self-perception and personal identity of the people responsible. As already noted, Regina's husband Barates, had travelled to Britain from his native Palmyra in Syria (p. 78). Despite being from southern Britain herself, Regina's depiction on her tombstone is reminiscent of Palmyrene art, showing her adorned with eastern jewellery and a diadem, and holding a spindle and distaff typical in Palmyrene art. She sits, however, in a high-backed wicker chair which was common to the north-western provinces, including Britain. Even the inscription is indicative of dual identity, the top section being written in Latin and the bottom in the script of Barates' native tongue. Here we see the expression of Palmyrene identity imposed within a foreign milieu, presumably by Barates, although as we saw, what may be Barates' own, more humble tombstone is much more traditionally 'Roman'. It becomes apparent that, on occasion, certain people chose to emphasize native characteristics, even if they had not moved away from their place of origin.

Two burial chests from Ephesus make this quite clear (p. 113). While stylistically they are closely related, perhaps even made by the same workshop, they were destined for very different people. The first one was made for a native family who had the chest inscribed in Latin, the official language of Asia Minor once it entered the empire, but quite tellingly, also in their native Greek. The second one, on the other hand, was the tomb of a soldier of the Seventh Praetorian Cohort (bodyguards of the emperor) who was born in Liguria, Italy, but was stationed in Ephesus. He chose only Latin to commemorate his life on the side of his tomb, but nevertheless it was decorated in a local style.

CHAPTER 4

SOMETHING TO BELIEVE IN

BEFORE THE ADOPTION of Christianity as the state religion of the empire in the early fourth century AD, the Romans had a particularly inclusive attitude towards almost all religious practices. As their armies and traders spread across Europe, North Africa and the Near East they took their gods and goddesses with them, the cults of which found new roots in far-off lands. Similarly, they encountered other faiths – some already familiar from past encounters with foreign cultures, some entirely new – and transported them either back to Rome or wherever else they continued to in their travels. The empire was bustling with gods, some worshipped in large public festivals in all corners of the known world, others honoured in secret by select groups of initiates behind closed doors. Evidence of these deities is everywhere in the archaeological record and ranges from the largest temples in major urban centres to names of the divine scratched on the simplest of pots and left at religious places by the most humble of inhabitants.

Above: This sandstone marker found in Egypt shows the emperor Diocletian in traditional royal dress and offering to the Buchis Bull, sometimes associated with the cult of the god Ra. Similar to the Birdoswald Hercules, it shows that the emperor could be included in any local religion of the Roman Empire. Upper Egypt, AD 288. H. 76.5 cm, W. 48 cm.

Although provincial temples of north-western Europe and North Africa appear architecturally different to those of Rome, their very existence is evidence of how much the religious landscape changed with the advance of the Romans. Several Roman authors such as Lucan (*The Civil War*, Book 3) and Dio Cassius (*Roman History* 62.7) describe the religion of native Gallic and British peoples as being conducted in open areas around natural features such as groves, caves and rivers, and involving 'savage rites', most notoriously human sacrifice. As discussed previously, the disdain expressed by some Romans towards the native peoples of these regions may well have led these authors to exaggerate. Emphasizing the alien aspects of these religions would have shocked and titillated their audiences back home, as well as aggrandizing themselves and their emperors for eradicating such barbarities and bringing civilization to wild and bloodthirsty peoples. However, it is certainly the case that, prior to Roman occupation, no religious structures can be identified archaeologically from most areas within these regions. Where Greek and Etruscan influence had impacted on parts of southern Gaul before the Romans, stone-built structures for religious centres are occasionally found, for example at Entremont and Roquepertuse. But these shrines are notably different from those of Rome and were often adorned with images of, and actual, severed human heads. Hoards of human limb bones were also discovered at the pre-Roman sanctuary at Ribemont-sur-Ancre.

In Gaul and Britain, the Roman period saw the wide-scale construction of wooden and stone structures imposed on the landscape for the primary purpose of religious worship. It was not only the homes of the gods that became more visible, but the very gods themselves. Images of deities carved in stone, cast in bronze or depicted in the mosaics that adorned rich buildings also developed only after the Roman conquest, though a few pre-Roman images, possibly of native deities carved from wood have survived. It is interesting that those gods depicted in the new art forms were primarily the new gods, while those of

Below: Altar dedicated to a native British hunter god, from Bisley-with-Lypiatt, Gloustershire, mid-1st–4th century AD. He is shown wearing a conical hat and short tunic, and holding a throwing stick and a hare. Limestone, H. 63 cm, W. 33 cm, D. 18.5 cm.

the Celtic peoples were only rarely represented. The numerous small bronze figurines encountered on Romano-British and Romano-Gallic sites are predominantly of recognizable Roman gods and goddesses and may have been used by worshippers in private household shrines or left as dedications at sanctuaries.

However, would a figurine of a bearded man in a classical pose that looks every bit like Jupiter to us, be recognized as Jupiter by an inhabitant of Roman Britain? The process of religious exchange was far more complex than simply bringing new gods to conquered regions and we must always be conscious of the religious heritage of the peoples within the empire and how this impacted on their perception of the many and diverse Roman gods.

Evidence for the spread and adoption of Roman gods in provincial areas takes many forms and varies between different parts of the empire depending on pre-existing traditions of religious worship.

Before the arrival of the Romans, the Iron Age peoples of Britain, Gaul and Germany had a vibrant religious pantheon of their own, populated by gods who had names – Sucellus, Toutates, Epona – and distinct physical appearances. One such god was shown sitting cross-legged with antlers sprouting from his head, another carried a wheel and a hammer. The Roman invaders and settlers brought with them their own gods, also with distinctive personalities and appearances, such as Jupiter, Minerva and Apollo. The ensuing melange resulted in a series of divine usurpations, conflations and even 'marriages' in what was described by Tacitus (*Germania* 43.4) as the *interpretatio romana*, the

Opposite top: Figurine of Cupid holding a quiver. Found at Falmer, East Sussex. Mid-1st–4th century AD. Bronze, H. 7.2 cm, W. 2 cm.

Opposite bottom: Figurine of Fortuna holding a horn of plenty (cornucopia) and an offering bowl (patera). Anzi, Italy, 1st–2nd century AD. Bronze, H. 11.1 cm.

Right: Figure of Jupiter holding a sceptre and a thunderbolt. Images of Roman gods borrowed heavily from Greek art. Hungary, 1st–2nd century AD. Bronze, H. 23.6 cm. W. 11 cm.

'Roman interpretation' of non-Roman gods. The classical Graeco-Roman image of Minerva dressed in helmet and *aegis* (a breastplate adorned with the head of Medusa) was adopted to represent the local British goddess Senuna, seen on golden votive 'leaves' from Ashwell in Hertfordshire. In Gaul, Mercury was 'married' to the Celtic goddess Rosmerta and the pair was worshipped together as shown on a series of altars.

Elsewhere in the empire, where divine images already had a history of visual representation, the influence of Rome is still seen. In Egypt – part of the Roman Empire since

Below: Disc showing the mythical twins Romulus and Remus being suckled by a wolf. The disc was found in London and shows a popular scene in classical Roman art. Mid-1st–4th century AD. Copper alloy, Diam. 8 cm.

Above: Figurine of a horse and rider, made in two parts, from Nottinghamshire. The motif of a horse and rider is common in British and Gallic art of this period and may relate to a native deity associated with Mars. 2nd–3rd century AD. Copper alloy, H. (horse) 7.3 cm, L. (horse) 9.3 cm, H. (rider) 6.6 cm, W. (rider) 4.4 cm.

Augustus' victory over Marc Antony in 31 BC – adoration of the ancient Egyptian gods continued unabated and their imagery, in general, changed very little. On occasion, however, a Roman 'makeover' is evident: statues of Horus, one of the most revered of the Egyptian gods, show him dressed not in his traditional kilt, but in Roman military attire (p. 11). This was a suitably literal transformation for the period since the god Horus represented the living king and that 'king' was now a Roman.

Worship of Egyptian gods positively flourished under the empire beyond the borders of Egypt itself. The cult of Isis, the powerful Egyptian mother goddess, had been growing in the Greek world since the conquest of Egypt by Alexander the Great and even reached Rome via Hellenistic traders. But under Roman control it spread even further across the imperial territories, carried with the movement of merchants, administrators and the army, and dedications and a possible temple to Isis have been discovered in London. This was not to everyone's liking. The emperor Tiberius is alleged to have had adherents of the cult crucified and statues of the goddess thrown into the Tiber, possibly in response to a sexual element of the cult that was distasteful to Roman sensibilities. Such a reaction from an emperor, however, is testament to the size of the cult which had grown to such a degree that it was considered a threat. Nonetheless, the worship of Isis continued to go from strength to strength and a small but highly decorative Roman temple to her has been preserved in Pompeii. Other deities from Egypt were also widely celebrated, in particular Serapis who was the consort of Isis and was associated with the ancient Egyptian god of the underworld, Osiris. Like the cult of Isis, the worship of Serapis initially spread out of Egypt during the Hellenistic period as part of a deliberate political strategy of the Ptolemaic rulers of Egypt to unify the Greek and Egyptian worlds. He was particularly favoured by the Flavian emperors of the late first century AD after Vespasian visited Alexandria and saw the huge Serapeum which had been constructed for the god's worship, before returning to Rome. Serapis also occasionally featured on the coins of the Flavian and Severan emperors, alongside the portrait of the emperor himself.

While images of the divine can tell us who was worshipped, rarer textual evidence can tell us how this was done. The survival of written texts that were not inscribed on durable materials is uncommon in north-western Europe where conditions are, for the most part, neither sufficiently wet nor sufficiently dry to ensure preservation of organic material. It is in the deserts of North Africa where this material survives and thousands of documents written on papyrus and other materials have been uncovered from Egypt. Many of these record spells, incantations and prayers to various gods and demons, asking for good things to befall the supplicants or bad things to befall their enemies. These, unlike the official calendar of public festivals, give us insight into the personal faiths and spiritual concerns of individuals living at the time.

While the perishable nature of most ancient writing materials means that their survival is restricted to only a few geographical regions, similar prayers and curses were also inscribed on sheets of lead. These are found all over the empire and, in general, indicate that the people of the Roman world had very similar attitudes about the divine's usefulness in cases of theft, love and even chariot racing. Prayers, or more usually vindictive curses, were inscribed on these sheets, rolled up and buried in the ground (sometimes in graves) or thrown into watery places. Over a hundred have been recovered from the famous Roman spring at Bath, and the similarity of these so-called *defixiones* to those from Greece, Rome and other provinces is remarkable.

One of the main concerns for which the divine were invoked was health. The cult of the Greek semi-divine healer Asklepios (to the Romans, Aesculapius) was particularly popular throughout the empire, and altars and statues to the god, with his distinctive staff entwined by a snake (still the symbol of the medical profession today) are known from northern Britain to Pergamon in modern Turkey and, of course, in his native Greece. One facet of this worship that survives in certain parts of the world to this day was the offering of miniature models of body parts in the temples of the god as a visual aid for identifying the afflicted organ. Model eyes are particularly common and the considerable attention paid by Greek and Roman medical professionals to conditions affecting sight – including detailed surgical instructions for the removal of cataracts (of course, without anaesthetic) – demonstrates that such problems of the eyes were common complaints. Model wombs are also frequently uncovered, perhaps indicative of problems in conceiving a child or complications in pregnancy.

For the western provinces, contact with the east (both within and beyond the empire) opened the gates for a flood of new gods. Gods from Egypt have already been mentioned, but in addition the great mother goddess Cybele arrived in her lion-drawn chariot from Phrygia, Mithras came from Zoroastrian Persia followed by his torch-bearers Cautes and Cautopates, and a prominent Baal god – later conflated with Jupiter and renamed Jupiter Dolichenus – crossed the empire standing atop his bull from Doliche in Asia Minor. These gods looked very different from those of Rome and the Celtic provinces (as far as we can tell what the latter looked like), and the exoticism of their appearance may have contributed to their religious aura. Their worship was, as far as the

Right: Anatomical votive in the shape of a breast. Italy, 2nd century BC. Terracotta, H. 5.3 cm, Diam. 8 cm.

limited evidence suggests, conducted in secret and only the initiated few could participate in the ceremonies. Where Mithraea – temples dedicated to the worship of Mithras – have been excavated across the empire, they frequently have sunken floors or are completely underground, adding to the sense of mystery and exclusivity surrounding the activities that were conducted within them. There are even reports of a secret handshake between initiates. We know that there were several grades of initiation, which are recorded on a number of archaeological discoveries, although how many grades there were and the precise nature or initiation ritual of each remains unclear. Most famously, images associated with the different grades are depicted on the mosaics from a Mithraeum at Ostia, just south-west of Rome, and the names of these ranks were inscribed on walls at the Syrian town of Dura Europos along with the names of local cult members. Overall, it seems that the rituals surrounding the worship of Mithras were as difficult for many Romans to understand as they are for us today. It appears, however, that the cult was particularly popular with the army, and Mithraea and altars to the god are commonly discovered in frontier regions, such as the *limes* of the Danube and Hadrian's Wall.

Opposite: Decorative enamel mount showing lions and griffins, found in London. The enamel work on this Roman mount is typical of pre-Roman Celtic art. 1st–4th century AD. Enamel and copper alloy, H. 17.8 cm, W. 13.3 cm.

The worship of Cybele allegedly required more than a secret handshake. Priests of her cult, known as Corybantes or Galli, were required to ritually castrate themselves in imitation of her mythical consort Attis, who severed his own genitals in grief after rejection by Cybele following a moment of infidelity. A strange object recovered from the River Thames and now in the British Museum's collection is adorned with images of Cybele and Attis along with many Graeco-Roman gods (p. 131). Its resemblance to modern horse emasculators has been noted and it may have been used for castration purposes by the Corybantes themselves.

Another exotic religion to be imported from the east was the cult of Jesus Christ, brought to Rome and the full extent of the empire by his followers, the Christians. However, unlike most other religious faiths, the Christians were viewed as a threat to the Roman Empire. This was because they, along with the Jews, refused to acknowledge any other gods but their own, not necessarily denying the existence of other supernatural beings but believing that they were no more than evil demons. Had the Christians at least been willing to recognize the divinity of the emperor himself, and by extension his absolute authority, they perhaps would not have had to endure the level of persecution that they suffered in the first three centuries AD. The cult of the emperor underpinned public religion throughout the Roman world. Dead emperors were, with a few exceptions, declared to be gods by their successors. The propagation of a cult which declared that the ruler of the empire was divine was a deliberate political tactic as it ensured the loyalty of the emperor's subjects. Though other cults, such as Mithraism, had monotheistic tendencies in the sense that they championed the worship of one god above all others, they were at least tolerant of the existence of other gods and, most importantly, of participation in the worship of the emperor. The Christians' refusal to acknowledge the emperor as divine was not

taken by the state as a sign of religious intolerance: it was treason and a declaration of political insurrection that could not go unpunished. The Christians, with their one god, were viewed with suspicion as a potentially unstable and rebellious social collective. This did have its benefits since they became a convenient scapegoat whenever the empire faced crisis: they no doubt continually brought disaster to the realm by offending the gods of the empire, particularly the one living in Rome. As a result, evidence for Christian worship before the fourth century is rare, coming from a few outspoken clerics such as Tertullian and famously the 'sator-rotas' cryptogram, the letters of which can be rearranged to read 'pater noster' (Our Father) twice in the form of a cross

Above: Romano-British 'face pot'. Almost all face pots have been found at military sites in Britain, Gaul and along the Rhineland. Their specific function is currently unknown but in some instances they were used as cremation urns. Provenance unknown, probably 1st–2nd century AD. Ceramic, H. 19.8 cm, Diam. (at mouth) 17.3 cm.

flanked by alpha and omega, the beginning and the end. Such evidence implies that their worship was conducted largely in secret, though out of concerns for personal safety rather than the exclusivity sought by the followers of Mithras.

In AD 313 the Edict of Milan, issued by Constantine the Great and his co-emperor Licinius, freed the Christians from persecution but only in so far as it offered toleration to all religions of the empire. The emperor himself remained *Pontifex Maximus* – the high priest of the non-Christian ('pagan') faiths – and was even declared a god himself upon his death. Over the course of the following centuries Constantine's successors gradually tightened the reins on the pagan religions of the empire until Theodosius I (r. AD 379–95) finally declared all public worship of pagan gods outlawed. Great churches were constructed, such as the original

Below: Serrated forceps decorated with busts of Cybele, Attis and other Greek and Roman gods. Found in the River Thames, London. Mid-1st–4th century AD. Bronze, L. 28 cm.

St Peter's in Vatican City and St Sophia in Istanbul, while pagan temples were abandoned, actively destroyed or used for a different purpose.

However, while imperial religion had changed to an unrecognizable degree, evidence of worship by ordinary people tells a more complex story. In Britain there are very

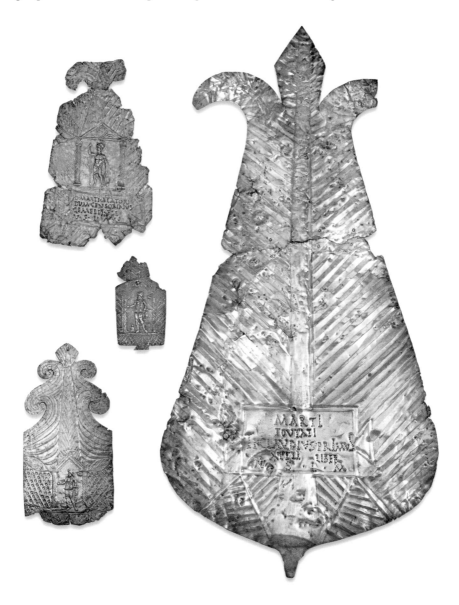

few buildings that can be identified as churches dating to the fourth century AD. The most convincing example is an annexed room in the Roman villa at Lullingstone, Kent, which was decorated with murals of people standing with arms raised in prayer around a large chi-rho, the early Christian monogram of Christ consisting of the first two letters of his name in Greek superimposed. Conversely, this period saw a flourish in the construction and renovation of pagan temples, particularly in the south-east of the province.

Other forms of evidence for early Christian worship in Britain can be found, notably personal objects such as lamps and items of jewellery decorated with chi-rho monograms. Most famously, a hoard of silverware discovered in Water Newton, Cambridgeshire in 1975 contained vessels inscribed with seemingly Christian messages and seventeen thin silver and gold plaques decorated in repoussé (where the design is beaten out from the reverse side) with lines resembling the veins of leaves or barbs of feathers. Most of these plaques bore a prominent chi-rho in the centre (p. 134). One also had an inscription stating that a woman named Anicilla had dedicated this plaque in the fulfilment of a vow. Interestingly, the idea of offering of an object of material value to the Christian god in thanks for assistance seems to be at odds with the Christian concept of divine grace. The Water Newton plaques can be better understood when viewed alongside typical pagan forms of worship since they are almost identical to a well-known form of pagan votive offerings, found in Britain and elsewhere in the empire, which were dedicated to various gods as a reward for answering some request on the part of the donor. These too were decorated to resemble leaves or feathers and bore an image of the god in question at their centre (left). The variants from the Water Newton Christian treasure merely replace the image of a pagan god with that of the Christian Jesus but were used and offered in the same manner. This implies that no strict division between Christian and pagan religious practice was observed among the population of

Opposite: Silver votive plaques. They are formed in the shape of elaborate leaves and often decorated with images of the gods and dedicatory inscriptions. Barkway, Hertfordshire, 3rd century AD. H. (max) 51.2 cm, (min) 8.95 cm. W. (max) 25.6 cm, (min) 4.76 cm.

Roman Britain, and possibly no strict division between
perceptions of the gods themselves.

Perhaps the best evidence for religious integration
within the empire is found among the ruins of the Syrian
town of Dura Europos, part of the empire for less than a

Opposite: Silver
votive plaque in the
shape of a stylized
leaf, embossed with
the Christian chi-rho
monogram. These
Christian plaques
appear to have evolved
from the earlier pagan
examples of similar
form, shown on page
132. Water Newton,
Cambridgeshire,
4th century AD.
Silver, L. 7 cm,
W. 5.2 cm.

hundred years in the second and third centuries AD. It was located right at the eastern edge of Roman territory, on the border with the powerful Sassanian Empire of Persia, which eventually captured the town in the mid-third century. It was positioned on the Euphrates river, along an important trade route between the east and the west, and as such, was heavily influenced by a diverse cultural mix. The remarkable preservation of buildings and artefacts from the town, known as 'the Pompeii of the desert', gives an insight into local culture that is not usually available to modern archaeologists. Among these are a series of buildings for religious use, with surviving wall paintings that tell us the cults and religions practised within the town. Within its relatively small area were discovered a Christian church and baptistery (the earliest known of its kind), a Jewish synagogue, a Mithraeum, a temple to Jupiter Dolichenus, a temple to the Palmyrene god Bel, as well as several others to various Greek, Roman and eastern deities. The number of religious institutions existing side-by-side in this town is testament to the religious vibrancy of the Roman world as a whole.

PART III: LEGACY

'YOU CHEER MY HEART BY
BUILDING SO, THAT ROME
SHALL BE ETERNAL'

PLUTARCH, *SAYINGS OF KINGS AND COMMANDERS* 208

THROUGHOUT THIS BOOK we have considered the impact of the Roman Empire on the lives of those who dwelt in and alongside it. From auxiliaries recruited in the deserts of Arabia and then transported to the furthest reaches of northern Britain, to female property owners in Egypt, the glimpses we have of these lives have intrigued and inspired people over the intervening centuries just as they do us today. This final chapter looks at the legacy of the concept of the power and people of Rome; not so much 'What have the Romans done for us?' but rather how the Romans continue to influence and inspire our thinking.

AT THE END of the fourth century AD the Roman Empire split in half when Theodosius I divided it between his two sons. These then became the Western Empire, with its capital at Ravenna in Italy (Rome having declined in importance) and the Eastern Empire, with its capital at Constantinople, modern Istanbul in Turkey. The Western Empire quickly fell to a succession of Germanic tribes known as the Vandals, the Goths and the Huns, and by the late fifth century AD the Romans had effectively lost control of this territory. The Eastern Empire, however, flourished, evolving into the Byzantine Empire. Though military and administrative control was lost or evolved beyond recognition, the borders of the Roman Empire continued to expand through its legacy and influence.

The Latin language, or to be more precise, the Vulgar Latin spoken by the non-elite members of the empire in the fourth and fifth centuries AD (which was less structured than formal Classical Latin) still underpins the basic structure of all modern Romance languages, including Spanish, Portuguese, French and, of course, Italian. The word 'Romance' itself comes from the Vulgar Latin *romanice*, roughly meaning 'in the Roman vernacular'. These languages are now spoken in parts of the world that the Romans never reached, such as South America, Canada and parts of southern and central Africa. Vulgar Latin was preserved throughout the ages, largely due to the Christian church, which adopted it for sermons in place of Classical Latin in order to communicate its message to the masses in a language that they would easily understand. English itself, though classified as a Germanic language, owes much to the Latin vernacular and both linguistic traditions have greatly influenced the modern English that we speak today. Often English will have several words for the same thing, since each will have a root in either Latin or Proto-Germanic languages; for example, 'help' (from Proto-Germanic *helpan*) and 'assist' (from the Latin *assistere*), or 'wage' (from Proto-Germanic *wadjojan*) and 'salary' (from Latin *salārium*). This is also the reason why often the adjective of a noun will sound nothing like it, such as 'town/urban', or 'water/ aquatic', the noun having a Germanic stem and the adjective a Latin one. Much of the Latin used in modern English arrived indirectly from Old French following the Norman conquest of England in 1066. Furthermore, in the Middle Ages Latin was the single language that could be understood by all educated Europeans and it was used as the lingua franca (common language) for law, medicine and the church: circles which still make extensive use of Latin today.

In addition to its language, many aspects of life in the Roman Empire are reflected in contemporary Western culture. With the constant movement of people over vast territories, the Roman Empire can be credited with creating the first truly multicultural society. The empire laid the foundations for travel around modern Europe, North Africa and the Near East both metaphorically and literally since many of its road systems are still in use. Watling Street, the Roman road that linked London to the channel crossings at Dover and Richborough, survives today as the A2. In general, cultural exchange and adoption was viewed favourably as it brought trade, imports and new fashions, but as we have seen it was also sometimes viewed with suspicion or hostility. The opinions expressed by Roman authors on the subject often reflect the complex issues surrounding migration in today's world. Individuals within the Roman Empire faced the same concerns as we do now – how to adapt to a new culture in an unfamiliar land and whether to embrace it or try to maintain their own traditions. Attitudes towards different faiths were similarly mixed and sometimes flared up in hostility. Generally the policy was one of acceptance and tolerance, but there were concerns about any elements of fundamentalism which could threaten to destabilize political power. Perhaps this is the reason why the Roman Empire continues to fascinate people today, because so much of it seems familiar. However, much does not just seem familiar but actually is still present. Western European urban lifestyles, legal systems, languages, money and even the existence of social benefits owe a great deal to Roman models.

Particularly in architecture, the legacy of the Romans continues today. Direct influences come from some of the most innovative yet nowadays most ubiquitous architectural techniques or models, which include the inventions of concrete, window glass, under-floor heating, or structures like the apartment building or the dome. Other influences, however, affect architectural style. During the Renaissance in Italy, architects rediscovered the old Roman building manuals, most importantly that by the architect Vitruvius, written in the first century BC. Only the text had been preserved, however, so the Italian architects started to make their own drawings based on that text. They then based their own sixteenth-century style on the Greek and Roman principles of symmetry, proportion and perspective that they read about, resulting in the architecture of the well-known Italian *palazzi*. The most famous of these architects was Andrea Palladio (1508–80), whose Palladian style, which evolved into what is called the neo-Palladian style, became popular in Britain, Germany and the United States in the seventeenth and eighteenth centuries. An early follower was the great British architect Inigo Jones, who based the design of the Queen's Chapel at St James's Palace on that of the

Pantheon, to evoke a Roman temple, and the design of the Palace of Whitehall on the Palladian *palazzo*.

These early examples of Roman-style buildings made way in the mid-eighteenth century for the neoclassical style, which spread through the whole of northern Europe as well as the Russian Empire and the United States. As a reaction to the extravagant Baroque style and at the time when newer archaeological discoveries were being made, such as the ruins of Pompeii and Herculaneum as well as more detailed studies of the ruins of Rome (as opposed to the sometimes fantastical reconstruction by the early Renaissance architects), the neoclassical style remained slightly more constrained than the neo-Palladian style. More importantly for us, it used the original Roman influence in a more academic and standardized way. Artists and architects visited Rome in order to study the monuments and ruins, then made their own reconstructions and used them to make models and designs in their home countries. Examples of such neoclassical buildings are all around us, some of the most famous being the Capitol in Washington DC (designed by William Thornton), the Pantheon in Paris (designed by Jacques-Germain Soufflot), the Altes Museum in Berlin (designed by Karl Friedrich Schinkel), the refurbishment of Catherine the Great's Palace in St Petersburg (by the Scottish architect Charles Cameron) and many others throughout the world. In fact, the façade of the British Museum itself (designed by Robert Smirke) is a product of that architecture, this time however, being modelled after a Greek rather than Roman building (p. 141).

Other ideas and concepts of the Roman Empire also fascinated the scholars of the eighteenth-century European Enlightenment. During this period, in which archaeology and other sciences were established and the arts flourished, the art, technology and especially the laws and government of the Roman Empire were topics of research and discussion for many. For example, writing during the period of the French Revolution, Constantin François de Chassebœuf, Comte de Volney considered in his philosophical history *Les Ruines, ou méditations sur les révolutions des empires* how powerful empires that seemed indestructible later failed and were overcome, using Rome as one model for his political and economic treatise on his own world. More famously, Gibbon's *Decline and Fall of the Roman Empire*, which was begun in 1776, examined the end of the empire in search of an explanation as to why it fell, describing 'the vicissitudes of fortune, which spares neither man nor the proudest of his works, which buries empires and cities in a common grave' (chapter 71). Works such as these tended to focus on the despotic nature of empire, reflecting the revolutionary spirit of the age in which they were written as much as exploring the empires that they study.

In the nineteenth century, in Britain at least, this view of the Roman Empire as a despotic institution began to change as the British acquired an empire of their own and looked to the power of Rome as a historic symbol and exemplar. The English word 'empire' itself comes from the Latin *imperium*, the word used to describe the power of the *imperator*, the 'emperor'. By the early twentieth century the ideology that the British Empire was the heir to its Roman predecessor had emerged and it was considered that the modern empire could learn both from the triumphs and from the ultimate downfall

POLY-OLBION

GREAT BRITAINE

By
Michaell Drayton
Esqr:

London printed for { M Lownes. I Browne. Cngraue
{ I Helme. I Busbie. } by W Hole.

of its ancient forebear. Thus we find that art and imagery from the Victorian period in Britain is full of references to the Romans.

The image of a female Britannia as a symbol of the British Empire and its empress Victoria is one which is familiar today, although the history of this is longer than many of us may realize. Imagery and descriptions of Elizabeth I alluded both to Britannia and that nemesis of the Romans, Boudicca (p. 143), as part of perceptions of her as the head of state and a virgin warrior queen. Even after Elizabeth's death this interest in Britannia continued, and amongst the characters in the pageants that took place to celebrate the accession of James I and his unification of England and Scotland into a nation named Great Brittaine, a 'fair and beautiful nymph, Britannia herself' is described. The title page of Michael Drayton's *Poly-Olbion* (15,000 lines of poetry describing the features of England and Wales), which was published in 1612, is among the first surviving depictions of a personified Britannia. She is shown on the title page of the book seated under an arch holding a sceptre and a cornucopia. Around sixty years after Drayton, during the reign of Charles II, Britannia made her first appearance on British coinage since the Roman period. She remained there until 2008. The original official seal of the Bank of England from its foundation in 1694 depicts 'Brittannia sitting looking on a Bank of Mony'.

The reign of Queen Victoria and the role of Britain as the holder of a naval empire saw Britannia remodelled to hold

a trident with a British lion at her feet and a Greek hoplite shield decorated with the union flag. Britannia has even inspired 'daughter' images for countries within the empire and now commonwealth. For example, Zealandia appeared on stamps in New Zealand in the early twentieth century and was also immortalized in marble statues as part of war memorials for the Boer War. She still features in the country's coat of arms. Not an outcome that the Romans could have ever expected.

Just as Elizabeth I was depicted as both Britannia and Boudicca, everywhere in Europe the art of the Romantic and Victorian periods contained references to the glory of the

Roman past, but equally the valour and independent spirit of those who challenged Rome as an oppressor. Caught in the spirit of Romanticism, each nation celebrated their heroes, individuals who fought social convention (in this case, 'Rome the oppressor') without regard for their own lives. In Great Britain, this was Boudicca; in France, Vercingetorix, who fought Caesar at Alesia; in Germany, Arminius who annihilated three Roman legions in the Teutoburg Forest; in Belgium, Ambiorix, chief of the Eburones, who fought Caesar, after which the tribe was wiped out. Statues of all of them, erected in that age of Romanticism, can be admired in their respective places of historic importance. Similarly, grand paintings by the leading artists of the day showed the same ideas and values (overleaf).

This fascination with Romantic figures continued into the twentieth century, albeit taking on a new form and on a different continent. In the Hollywood of the 1950s and 1960s

Right: The Hermannsdenkmal in Ostwestfalen-Lippe in Germany: a statue of the Romantic hero Arminius, who resisted the oppressor Rome in the Teutoburg Forest. Statue completed in 1875. Sandstone, iron pipe with copper plates, H. 53.46 m.

many epic movies and costume dramas were set in ancient Rome or the Roman Empire. During the 1950s many of these were based on novels that had been written at the end of the Victorian age; with the modern techniques of the time they could finally be translated onto the screen with all the pomp and glory with which they were conceived. The most famous of these films are probably *Quo Vadis?* (written in 1896 by Henryk Sienkiewicz, film 1951), *Ben-Hur* (written in 1880 by Lew Wallace, film 1959) and *The Last Days of Pompeii* (written in 1834 by Edward Bulwer-Lytton, film 1959), all of which are centred on the idea of the Romantic hero who defies social conventions and norms, but are converted into a Christian narrative in the Victorian period.

Encouraged by their popularity, production companies turned out more and sometimes even grander films, based on historical novels of the time or on original screenplays, often spiced up with the debauchery, corruption and larger-than-life personalities that people associated with the Romans.

Above: Thusnelda, Arminius' wife, is shown here as a prisoner of war in a triumphal parade in Rome. Her Victorian attire, as well as her proud and defiant attitude, associate her with the Romantic notion of rebellion against the Roman oppressor. Carl Theodor von Piloty, Thusnelda led in Germanicus' Triumph, 1873. Oil on canvas, 490 x 710 cm.

Among those set in ancient Rome are *The Robe* (1953), *Spartacus* (1960), *The Fall of the Roman Empire* (1964) and the most ambitious and grandest of all, *Cleopatra* (1963) – at the time the most expensive film to have ever been made. Fellini's controversial film *Satyricon* (1969) can also be placed in this series, perhaps as a culmination of the trend or perhaps as a parody of it, with over-the-top performances and scenes of ultimate decadence and perversion. In the following decades there were no more grand productions, no more epic stories (a lack of money in Hollywood being one cause), and the Roman Empire seems to have lost its appeal in cinema. The only exceptions of productions that enjoyed success at the time are *Monty Python's Life of Brian* (1979) and the BBC series *I, Claudius* (1976), based on the famous books by Robert Graves, who himself based them on the writings of the Roman author Suetonius (second century AD).

Recently, however, a spectacular surge has taken place in films and television series set in the Roman Empire. At the basis of this fascination lies the success of *Gladiator* (2000) which, very much in the tradition of the old epic movies, centres on the Romantic hero and uses splendour, pomp and mass scenes (now often computer generated) to achieve its

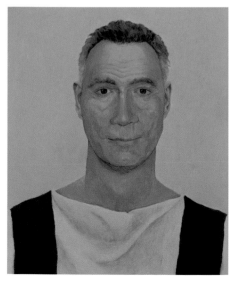

Below: With the developing technique of facial reconstruction, it is possible to see what individual Romans may have looked like. This illustration shows a man whose remains were excavated from a Roman-period burial near Bristol.

goal. One of the noticeable aspects of many of the newer productions is the way in which the Roman Empire is often correctly portrayed as a multicultural society of very different, sometimes non-Roman peoples. Thus, in *Gladiator*, the protagonist Maximus Decimus Meridius is a general in the Roman army, Spanish in origin, who is fighting the Germanic tribes in Germania and has never set foot in Rome. In *King Arthur* (2004), Arthur is portrayed as a fifth-century cavalry officer in Britannia, originally from Sarmatia (modern Ukraine, bordering ancient Dacia), fighting the Britons in his native Sarmatian armour for the Roman army. None of his fellow knights has ever seen Rome; Arthur himself has been once. Recently, two films inspired by the disappearance of the Ninth Legion (which originated in Spain) in Britannia have also been released: *Centurion* (2010) and *The Eagle* (2011). The same popularity is also reflected on television where series such as *Rome* (2005–2007) and *Spartacus* (2010–present) have enjoyed enormous success.

Even earlier than in film, the idea of Rome and the Roman Empire had already been explored through literature for many centuries. William Shakespeare set five plays in ancient Rome and brought, among others, the stories of Julius Caesar and Antony and Cleopatra to Elizabethan and Jacobean London, while his contemporary Ben Jonson was arrested following his play about Lucius Aelius Sejanus (a favourite of the emperor Tiberius), as it was seen as an allegory for corruption at the court of James I. More modern playwrights including Henrik Ibsen (*Emperor and Galilean*, 1873) and Albert Camus (*Caligula*, 1944) have also explored imperial Roman characters and settings as allegories for contemporary society. Writers including Lord Byron and Edgar Allan Poe wrote poetry inspired by their visits to the ancient sites of Rome, while Rudyard Kipling's poem, 'The Roman Centurion's Song' imagines the feelings of a soldier who has been based in Britain for forty years on being ordered back to Rome.

So many novelists have found rich material in the Roman world that it would be impossible to mention them all, but they stretch from Sienkiewicz's 1896 *Quo Vadis*, referred to above, to much more recent publications such as Colleen McCullough's series *Masters of Rome* (1990–2007) or Robert Harris' *Pompeii* (2003) and *Imperium* (2006). Unlikely as it might sound, the Roman Empire has inspired several series of detective fiction too, including Lindsey Davis' Marcus Didius Falco books and Steven Saylor's *Roma sub Rosa* series. Caroline Lawrence has written the *Roman Mysteries* series for children, and of course whole generations have grown up enjoying the Asterix comics by René Goscinny and Albert Uderzo.

The characters and settings of all of these works, from Shakespeare to Asterix to *Gladiator*, chime with us in a way that so many other historical periods fail to do. Whether it is the familiarity of unsanitary public toilets and ever-rising taxes, or the drama of wars and tragic love stories, something about Rome captures our imaginations over and over again in novels, poetry, plays and film.

The memory of Rome and the Roman Empire, whether pursued through academic research into historical events, or inspiring artists, writers and political thinkers, continues to thrive and has spread to parts of the globe untouched by the Romans themselves. The impact of the Romans may be obvious, appearing on our screens or public monuments, or it can be subtle, in our language and cultural norms. The vast output of Roman authors has ensured that a wealth of information about their lives and times has survived through the ages, and their own tendency to put a good story before reasonable fact has produced scores of familiar characters and well-known heroes and villains who continue to fire imaginations. Perhaps more than the physical remains themselves, the fascination of the Roman Empire lies in the stories of its people, from emperors to slaves. To this day, the distinguished and mighty culture of Rome continues to inspire us.

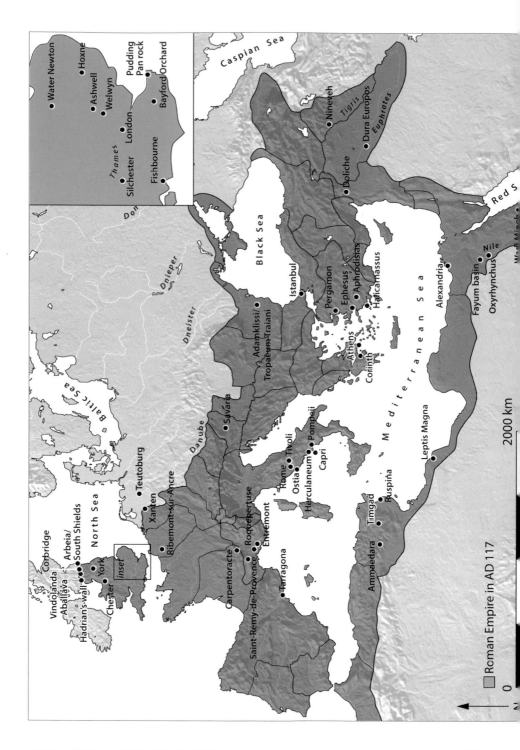

Water Newton
Hoxne
Ashwell
Welwyn
Pudding
Pan rock
London
Bayford Orchard
Thames
Silchester
Fishbourne
Don

Caspian Sea

Nineveh
Tigris
Dura Europos
Euphrates
Doliche

Red Sea

Black Sea

Istanbul
Pergamon
Ephesus
Aphrodisias
Halicarnassus

Alexandria
Nile
Fayum basin
Oxyrhynchus

Adamklissi/
Tropaeum Traiani

Athens
Corinth

Mediterranean Sea

Dnieper

Dneister

Savária

Danube

Leptis Magna

Rome
Tivoli
Ostia
Pompeii
Herculaneum
Capri

Teutoburg

Xanten

Ruspina

Baltic Sea

Ribemont-sur-Ancre

Roquepertuse
Entremont

Timgad

North Sea

Carpentoracte

Corbridge
Arbeia/
South Shields
Vindolanda
Aballava
Hadrian's Wall
Chester
York
inset

Saint-Rémy-de-Provence

Tarragona

Ammaedara

Roman Empire in AD 117

2000 km

0

N

ROMAN EMPIRE: POWER AND PEOPLE

List of sources

Abbreviations

CIL III = Mommsen, T. H. (ed.), *Corpus Inscriptionum Latinarum III. Inscriptiones Asiae, provinciarum Europae Graecarum, Illyrici Latinae* (Berlin, 1958).
CIL VIII = Mommsen, T. H. (ed.), *Corpus Inscriptionum Latinarum VIII. Inscriptiones Africae Latinae* (Berlin 1960).
ILS = Dessau, H., *Inscriptiones Latinae Selectae* (Berlin, 1902).
RIB = Collingwood, R. G. and R. P. Wright, *The Roman Inscriptions of Britain* (Oxford, 1965).
SHA = *Scriptores Historiae Augustae*

Ancient sources

Unless otherwise stated in the text, translations of ancient works are provided by Dirk Booms.

Aelius Aristides, *Orations 26: In Praise of Rome*
Caesar, *Gallic Wars* 1.1; 4.20
Cicero, *Against Verres* 2.2
Cicero, *For Marcus Fonteius* 11
Cicero, *Letters to Friends* 7.7
Dio Cassius, *Roman History* 62.7
Josephus, *The Jewish War* 3.5.7 (=3.107)
Livy, *History of Rome* 25.40.2
Lucan, *The Civil War*, Book 3
Marcus Aurelius, *Meditations* 7.49
Pliny the Elder, *Natural History* 6.84; 14.2; 37.18–22
Plutarch, *Sayings of Kings and Commanders* 208
Seneca, *On Clemency* 1.24.1
Scriptores Historiae Augustae, Hadrian 11.2
Statius, *Silvae* 4.5
Strabo, *Geography* 4.5.2
Suetonius, *Nero* 31.2
Tacitus, *Agricola* 12; 21.2
Tacitus, *Annals* 4.5; 14.44; 15.42.1
Tacitus, *Germania* 43.4

Above: Bust of a young boy. Dating to the 1st century AD. Provenance unknown. Marble, H. 33 cm.

Opposite: Map showing the cities mentioned in the text.

Modern sources

Davies, R. W., *Service in the Roman Army*, 11 (New York, 1989).
Gibbon, E., *The History of the Decline and Fall of the Roman Empire*, chapter 71 (London, 1776–89).
Sheldon, J., *As the Romans Did: A Sourcebook in Roman Social History*, 254 (Oxford, 1998).
Vindolanda Tablets Online, vindolanda.csad.ox.ac.uk: translations of Tablets 302, 346 and 628 © Centre for the Study of Ancient Documents, The British Museum and other copyright holders.

Further reading

Beard, M., *The Roman Triumph* (Harvard, 2009).

Bowman, A., *Life and Letters on the Roman Frontier* (London, 1994).

Clauss, M., *The Roman cult of Mithras: the god and his mysteries* (Oxford, 2001).

Connolly, P. and Dodge, H., *The Ancient City: Life in Classical Athens and Rome* (New York, 2000).

Erdkamp, P., *Blackwell Companion to the Roman Army* (San Francisco, 2007).

Hobbs, R. and Jackson, R., *Roman Britain: Life at the Edge of Empire* (London, 2010).

Irwin, D., *Neoclassicism* (London, 1997).

Judd, T., 'The Trade with India through the Eastern Desert of Egypt under the Roman Empire' (http://archaeology-easterndesert.com/assets/applets/LYSA_Judd.pdf).

King, A., *Roman Gaul and Germany* (London, 1990).

Opper, T., *Hadrian, Empire and Conflict* (London, 2008).

Potter, T. W. and Johns, C., *Roman Britain* (London, 2002).

Ramage, N. H. and Ramage, A., *British Museum Concise Introduction: Ancient Rome* (London, 2008).

Rives, J. B., *Religion in the Roman Empire* (San Francisco, 2007).

Tomber, R., 'From the Roman Red Sea to beyond the Empire: Egyptian Ports and their Trading Partners' in *British Museum Studies in Ancient Egypt and Sudan* 18 (2012): 201–215.

Wells, P. S., *The Barbarians Speak* (Princeton, 1990).

Woolf, G., *Becoming Roman: The Origins of Provincial Civilisation in Gaul* (Cambridge, 1998).

Wyke, M., *Projecting the Past: Ancient Rome, Cinema and History* (London, 1997).

Image credits

All photographs from the British Museum are © The Trustees of the British Museum. British Museum object registration numbers are listed below. Further information about the Museum and its collection can be found at britishmuseum.org.

p. 2   British Museum 1805,0703.436
p. 6   British Museum 1926,0416.1
p. 8   Map drawn by Craig Williams
p. 9 (above)   British Museum 1986,1001.64
p. 9 (below)   British Museum 1926,0416.1
p. 10   British Museum EA 53913
p. 11   British Museum 1912,0608.109
p. 12   British Museum CM R.10762
p. 14   British Museum 1855,0306.18 (Donated by Chambers Hall)
p. 17   British Museum 1971,0419.1 (Donated by The Art Fund in honour of David Robert Alexander Lindsay, 28th Earl of Crawford and 11th Earl of Balcarres)
p. 18 (above)   British Museum 1914,0627.1
p. 18 (below)   Aquarelle de Jean-Claude Golvin. Musée départemental Arles antique. © éditions Errance
p. 19   British Museum 1855,0306.18 (Donated by Chambers Hall)
p. 20   British Museum 1908,0417.5
p. 21 (above)   Aquarelle de Jean-Claude Golvin. Musée départemental Arles antique. © éditions Errance
p. 21 (below)   British Museum 1775,0616.1 (Donated by Sir William Hamilton)
p. 22   British Museum Images 00201570001
p. 23   British Museum 1872,1226.3 (Bequeathed by Felix Slade)
p. 24   British Museum 1931,0413.1 (Donated by Frank Neilson through the Art Fund)
p. 25   Map drawn by Craig Williams
p. 26 (above)   © Yale University Art Gallery Dura-Europos Collection 1933.715
p. 26 (below)   © Norwich Castle Museum NWHCM:1947.152:A
p. 27   UIG via Getty Images
p. 28   UIG via Getty Images
p. 29 (above)   Reconstruction drawing by Alan Sorrell. © English Heritage
p. 29 (below)   Roger Clegg
p. 30   © Tyne & Wear Archives & Museums / The Bridgeman Art Library
p. 31   LVR-Archaeological Park Xanten / LVR-RömerMuseum. Photographer Axel Thünker DGPh. Illustrator Sebastian Simonis
p. 32   British Museum 1857,0718.1
p. 33   British Museum 1873,0505.1
p. 34   British Museum 1911,0206.1 (Donated by J. A. Acton)

p. 35 (above)   British Museum 1856,0701.2
p. 35 (below)   British Museum 1935,0112.1
p. 36   British Museum 1856,0701.5
p. 37   British Museum 1856,0701.4
p. 38   © Bayerisches Landesamt für Denkmalpflege, Archiv-Nr. 1Ds09247 vom 19. Juni 2008, Photo: Klaus Leidorf
p. 39   © Deutsche Limeskommission, P. Henrich
p. 40   British Museum 1805,0703.106
p. 44 (left and right)   British Museum 1864,1128.261 (Donated by Edward Wigan)
p. 45 (above)   British Museum CM R.10300
p. 45 (below left and right)   British Museum CM R.10762
p. 46 (above)   British Museum 1872,0709.524
p. 46 (below left and right)   British Museum 1864,1128.61 (Donated by Edward Wigan)
p. 47   New York University Excavations at Aphrodisias (Guido Petruccioli)
p. 48   British Museum 1862,0616.1
p. 49 (left and right)   British Museum 1928,0208.2 (Donated by Worshipful Company of Goldsmiths, Calouste Sarkis Gulbenkian, Henry Van de Bergh and The Art Fund)
p. 50   British Museum 1988,0627.476
p. 51 (left)   British Museum 1919,0213.179 (Donated by Sir Arthur John Evans)
p. 51 (right)   British Museum 2002,0102.2969 (Bequeathed by Charles A. Hersh)
p. 53   Copyright Reading Museum (Reading Borough Council). All rights reserved
p. 54   British Museum 1805,0703.78
p. 57   British Museum 1807,0511.1 (Donated by Hon. Mrs Anne Seymour Damer)
p. 58   British Museum 1805,0703.106
p. 60   New York University Excavations at Aphrodisias (Guido Petruccioli)
p. 61   British Museum 1990,1004.1; 1856,0701.20; 1874,0328.42
p. 63   British Museum 1858,0819.1
p. 64   British Museum 1895,0408.1 (Donated by Sir Augustus Wollaston Franks)
p. 67   British Museum 1884,1215.1 (Donated by Ernest H Willett)
p. 70   British Museum 1813,1211.2 (Donated by George Kenyon, 2nd Baron Kenyon)
p. 73   Generaldirektion Kulturelles Erbe Rheinland-Pfalz, Landesarchäologie, Außenstelle Koblenz; Photos: W. Baumann
pp. 74–5   Alessandro0770/CrystalGraphics.com
p. 76   British Museum 1895,0408.1 (Donated by Sir Augustus Wollaston Franks)
p. 78   © Tyne & Wear Archives & Museums / The Bridgeman Art Library
p. 80   Yale University Art Gallery Dura-Europos Collection

Index